Happiness *for* Two

Happiness *for* Two

75 SECRETS
FOR FINDING
MORE JOY TOGETHER

Alexandra Stoddard

 Collins

An Imprint of HarperCollins*Publishers*

HarperCollins books may be purchased for educational, business, or sales promotional use. For information, please write: Special Markets Department, HarperCollins Publishers, 10 East 53rd Street, New York, NY 10022.

FIRST EDITION

Designed by Lorie Pagnozzi

Library of Congress Cataloging-in-Publication Data
Stoddard, Alexandra.
  Happiness for two : 75 secrets for finding more joy together / Alexandra Stoddard. - 1st ed.
        p. cm.
  Includes bibliographical references.
  ISBN 978-0-06-143563-8
  1. Happiness. 2. Couples-Psychology I. Title
  BF575.H27S765 2007
  646.7'8-dc22

07 08 09 10   ID2/RRD   10 9 8 7 6 5 4 3 2 1

PETER,

YOU ARE THE LOVE OF MY LIFE. EVERY DAY WE ARE
TOGETHER, IN LOVE, IS A PRIVILEGE AND A BLESSING.
BECAUSE WE HAVE ACHIEVED HAPPINESS FOR TWO,
I COULD HOPE FOR NOTHING MORE.

I CELEBRATE YOU, HONOR YOU, LOVE YOU,
AND WILL, FOREVER AND BEYOND.

THERE IS ONLY ONE
HAPPINESS IN LIFE,
TO LOVE AND BE LOVED.

George Sand

Contents

ACKNOWLEDGMENTS XIII

AN INVITATION TO HAPPINESS TOGETHER
BY PETER MEGARGEE BROWN XV

1. Treat Each Encounter as Though It Could Be Your Last 1

2. My Mantra: Love & Live Happy 3

3. Live at Ten 6

4. Pay Attention 9

5. Read Some Quality Literature Regularly 12

6. Go on Vacations Alone, Together 15

7. Assume More Responsibility at Home 17

8. Have 50–50 Voting Power 20

9. Criticize with Kindness 22

10. Encourage Each Other to Do Something Every Day That Will Boost Happiness 24

11. No Awkward Surprises 27

12. Together, Explore Your Spirituality 30

13. Write Each Other's New Year's Resolutions 33

14. Celebrate More 37

15. Work Daily on Your Character 40

16. Begin Each Encounter with a Smile 48

17. Don't Let Children Control You 51

18. Listen with a Third Ear 54

19. It's Okay to Agree to Disagree 57

20. Nurture Your Core Identity 59

21. Surround Yourselves with Mutual Friends 62

22. Don't Discuss Your Intimacy and Secrets with Others   65

23. Be There as a Support for All Important Occasions   67

24. A Home Has No Boss   69

25. It Feels Good to Look Good   71

26. When You Are Together, Be Together   74

27. Take Care of Your Own Health   76

28. Share Sensuous Meal Preparation   79

29. Encourage Adventures   81

30. Temper Your Temper   84

31. Run Errands Together   87

32. White Lies Are Always Dangerous   89

33. Write Love Notes   91

34. Give the Gift of Eye Contact   94

35. Mess Up, Clean Up   96

36. Offer to Help   98

37. Establish Your Own Rituals and Traditions   100

38. Stop Disappearing   102

39. Keep Business and Personal Affairs in Order   104

40. Allow Each Other Freedom for Contemplation   106

41. When Necessary, Be the Nurse   109

42. Bring Flowers Home   111

43. Talk Up, Not Down   114

44. Stop the Teasing   118

45. Sincerely Say You're Sorry   119

46. Encourage Each Other to Have More Fun   121

47. Don't Move Things from Each Other's Personal Spaces   124

48. Encourage Self-Expression   126

49. When Treats Become Traps   131

50. Remember Important Dates   134

51. Women Like to Talk Things Out   136

52. Don't Correct Each Other in Public   138

53. Generous Compliments Lighten the Heart   140

54. Explore Together Your Invisible Wealth   143

55. Don't Discuss Weight   147

56. Try Not to Interrupt   149

57. Tit-for-Tat Is Tiresome   151

58. Conversations Shouldn't Be Monologues   153

59. Be More Sentimental and Indulge Each Other   155

60. Never Pick a Fight   158

61. Please Don't Say Something You'll Regret   161

62. Play to Each Other's Strengths   163

63. Set Aside Certain Times for Serious Discussions   165

64. Control Your Tone   167

65. Grumpiness Is Contagious   169

66. Say "It's Okay"   172

67. Patience, Patience   174

68. Discover and Rediscover Each Other's Passions 176

69. Eat as Many Meals Together as Possible   179

70. Set Aside Times to Sit and Read Together   181

71. Stimulate Your Curiosity   184

72. Kindness and Diplomacy Win Hearts and Minds   187

73. Live a Little!   190

74. Me & You   192

75. Your Happiness Is Up to You   195

AFTERWORD   199

Acknowledgments

My life's great richness is due to my being a writer. I thank my friend and literary agent Carl Brandt for recognizing this *is* my life. I appreciate my editor, Toni Sciarra, for understanding my need to write books and for her help in the process of publication. You both care deeply about my work. I couldn't be who I am without your support, encouragement, brilliant minds, and thoughtful help every step of my journey.

I send you, Carl, and you, Toni, great affection, appreciation, happiness, and love.

An Invitation
to Happiness Together

I am a witness for over fifty-four years—and thirty-four years of marriage—to Alexandra's own remarkable development of strong character and achievement—as an interior designer, author, and lifestyle philosopher, who now presents her pioneering discovery of the essential keys to ways lovers can find greater joy in their lives. *Happiness for Two* is the delicious result.

My first observation began one sunny day in Southport, Connecticut. My sister Bebe introduced me to her young tennis partner on the court at the annual Labor Day tournament. Alexandra demonstrated then as a teenager a certain vigorous grace and bright spirit while playing the game with strength, laughter, and joy. At the same time, I noted that she and my sister managed, artfully, to win game after game, set after set, until they whipped their traumatized opponents royally and were awarded the coveted Silver Trophy.

That was a grand match in 1954 . . . Twenty years later, Alexandra and I were married at St. James' Church in Manhattan. We have been happily together ever since.

In between, Alexandra had graduated from Mary Burnham boarding school in Northampton, further honing her skills in interior design and tennis. Her art teacher, Phyl Gardner, played a significant role in persuading her not to apply to nearby Smith College and instead seek admission to the New York School of Interior Design, where she received the first full scholarship.

Alexandra's Aunt Betty, an international social worker, whisked her away for a trip around the world in 1959. It was a vivid, eye-opening experience, exposing her to architecture, design, and beauty as well as to scenes of sorrow, suffering, and poverty. The combination gave depth to her future design and literary careers, while increasing her understanding of human nature and our universal search for meaning and purpose in our lives.

When Alexandra returned to interior design school, she had the good fortune to meet Eleanor McMillen Brown (no relation), doyenne of interior design, who had come to the school to lecture. Alexandra was captivated by this brilliant seventy-year-old's exceptional grace and practical wisdom. With immediate appreciation of Alexandra's talent, Mrs. Brown hired her at the prominent firm McMillen, Inc.

Alexandra became Mrs. Brown's friend and special assistant. She worked there for fourteen years until her boss retired in 1977. Alexandra then decided to start her own interior design company, Alexandra Stoddard, Incorporated, with Mrs. Brown's blessings.

On Valentine's Day, 2007, as I often would do, I wrote a letter to Alexandra to tell her of my love for her these thirty-three years together—our own happiness for two. I told her how grateful I have been for her cheerful, creative spirit, high character, and achievement that have so blessed our lives. This, I said, had been an astonishing adventure that I wished to continue to share with her for all time.

Alexandra's compassionate, authentic book *Happiness for Two* tells a fresh and honest story, teaching all of us the gentle, incisive ways of being that enable lovers to grow more deeply in love, individually and together, throughout their lives, to find for themselves and experience happiness for two.

Alexandra's mantra: "Love & Live Happy."

Peter Megargee Brown

Happiness *for* Two

Treat Each Encounter as Though It Could Be Your Last

EACH DAY SHOULD BE PASSED AS
THOUGH IT WERE OUR LAST.

Publilius Syrus

When we think of each encounter as though it could be the last, there is a poetic tenderness that perfumes the atmosphere. We're living in the post–9/11 era, with a raised consciousness about how vulnerable we are. We never know if we will ever see each other again. The wisest way to keep our love fresh is to be aware of how deeply intertwined our lives are. When we live in the heart of each moment together, if and when our lover is taken from us, we will have few regrets.

What would you do differently if this moment together were your last? Think of someone you love who has died. Do you remember the last time you were together? Do you recall what you said and did?

We should keep our relationship up-to-date, moment by moment. It doesn't matter where we are or what the circumstances are as long as we're together. Now, remind yourself, you have each other and can hold each other affectionately. This acute awareness of the fragility of our love affair should change the way we think and act. Now may be the only time we have.

From this day forward, gently enjoy the sacred bond between you.

Whenever we live in this consciousness, it sparks the flames of love and intensifies our appreciation of the moment and of the shortness of life on earth.

I have found sublime happiness with Peter. I know this paradise on earth will not last forever. I'm aware at the same time that the energy of love never dies. While we have this blessing of our love for each other, we intend to treasure every moment we're privileged to be alive, in love, and together.

It is my fervent wish for you that each time you are with your lover, you will know anew how rare your happiness is, and your heart will overflow with appreciation.

When two souls in love meet and find happiness for two, this is the greatest blessing we can have bestowed upon us on this fleeting earthly journey. With all our relationships, when we understand each encounter as though it could be our last, we honor ourselves and others. See the light in your lover and others and openly express your gratitude and love.

> TREASURE EACH OTHER IN
> THE RECOGNITION THAT WE
> DO NOT KNOW HOW LONG
> WE SHALL HAVE EACH OTHER.
>
> **Joshua Loth Liebman**

2

My Mantra: Love & Live Happy

LOVE IS THE ULTIMATE AND
HIGHEST GOAL TO WHICH ONE CAN
ASPIRE. THE SALVATION OF
HUMANITY IS THROUGH LOVE AND
IN LOVE.

Viktor E. Frankl

The ultimate expression of fulfillment in a human life is to love another as your other self and through this precious bond find lasting happiness. Love is our life force, what I call our spirit-energy. We cannot live fully without loving and being loved. Love is the cornerstone of all well-being, all happiness. We're healed, supported, uplifted, and sustained by this greatest force for good.

For over thirty years, my mantra has been "Love & Live Happy." I find the words sacred, expressing mystical potentialities. Whenever I feel my spirit-energy of happiness deflating, I repeat my mantra: "Love & Live Happy." Love is the beginning, middle, and end of all our positive emotions. It is the foundation of all our profound feelings that are essential to increase our own happiness and the well-being of others.

Happiness for two requires two sensitive, loving souls who understand their own potential for wholeness individually. As a teenager I read Erich Fromm's classic, *The Art of Loving*. He taught that love is the only sane and satisfactory answer to the puzzle of human existence: "Satisfaction in individual love cannot be attained without the capacity to love one's neighbor, without true humility, courage, faith, and discipline."

Self-love, when properly understood, is the basis for love and happiness. If we don't have affection toward ourself, how are we able to love and understand others? When we accept and appreciate our own being, then we're ready to love life more abundantly, to pursue and achieve happiness for ourselves, and to inspire others to greater self-awareness and happiness.

When we love another person as our soul mate, we should continuously be aware of our thoughts as reflective of our partner's state of mind. I try to think of Peter as myself. Fundamentally, what I want and need is what he wants and needs. How I want to be loved and cherished is how he wants to be loved and cherished. We can then share more joy together.

Our motivation is to give unconditional love to our lover. Pure love requires empathy and the ability to put yourself in someone else's shoes, to see things from other people's point of view.

Whenever we focus on the good of others, the quality of our love and our compassion increases. True inner peace and happiness grow from cultivating a loving frame of mind. When we're able to think the most loving thoughts about others, we're able to control and transform our mind, gaining in wisdom. We become enlightened. Meditating each day on love fills our hearts with loving kindness. Love is not angry, jealous, or envious.

All happiness is dependent on our self knowledge, self-love, and the ability to extend this love to others. All our attempts to find lasting happiness in material objects will fail. We live from the inside out. Cultivating our ability to love our neighbor as ourselves is a great human accomplishment. When we love with this loving kindness, patience, and wisdom, we will find great happiness.

The more we love our own life, the more we inspire and strengthen our partner's journey. When we live in the spirit-energy of love, we are kinder, more sensitive, recognizing all the great qualities that attract us to each other. We will be more fully present for our lover.

Try this love meditation: Identify all the things you love about yourself, your lover, your parents, your grandparents, your children, your grandchildren, your friends, your neighbors, your pets, and the world. Be specific. What do you love most in nature? In human nature? What kinds of beauty uplift you? When we live in love and dwell in love, we nourish our soul. We free ourself. "Love & Live Happy," and share blessings with the world.

LOVE AND HAPPINESS ARE INEFFABLE
DIVINE MYSTERIES. SOME
EMOTIONS CAN'T BE DISSECTED. ONCE
YOU TAKE SOMETHING APART TO
ANALYZE COMPONENTS THEY DON'T
TICK ANYMORE.

Peter Megargee Brown

Live at Ten

BEING DEEPLY LOVED BY
SOMEONE GIVES YOU STRENGTH,
WHILE LOVING SOMEONE DEEPLY
GIVES YOU COURAGE.

Lao Tzu

In my book *Choosing Happiness*, I asked readers to use a scale of one to ten to determine their natural set-point of happiness. Doctors ask their patients to rate their pain levels from one to ten; why not use the same method to measure pleasure, satisfaction, and happiness? Think of ten as 100 percent, the best possible score.

In *Choosing Happiness* I suggested that our happiness set-point is determined 50 percent by nature and 50 percent by nurture. This theory has been verified by the latest scientific research. We're born with a certain temperament. This genetic inheritance accounts for approximately 50 percent of who we are. The other 50 percent is influenced by environment, by how we choose happiness, how we aim our lives toward avoiding suffering for ourselves and others through the shaping of our thoughts and actions toward the greatest good.

What is your natural set-point of happiness? Has it improved as you share happiness for two? Do you feel you both are stretching yourselves to the highest levels of love, understanding, and forgiveness? Aristotle taught us that it isn't life we should value, but the good life, the life well lived.

Life is short. Why wouldn't we want to go over the top in vitality, love, and achievement? Remember the words posted at the entrance of Zen temples:

> Let us be respectfully reminded:
> Life and death are of supreme
> importance. Time swiftly passes
> by and with it our only chance.
> Each of us must aspire to awaken.
> Be aware: Do not squander your life.

We live with no time out. The heart is beating and the clock is ticking. This is our only chance to awaken. Before you can take charge of your lives together, you have to work on yourself to notch up *your* set-point of happiness. No one can do our inner work for us. You are your own responsibility. Take the best possible care of yourself. Gain in self-knowledge. Express yourself with enthusiasm and confidence. Know and be true to your highest, happiest self. Be alert to all kinds of beauty around you and inside you. Find your passion and increase your commitment to expressing yourself in ways that benefit others. Say no to anything that could harm another person. Value your own happiness as your highest achievement.

Be mindful of your generosity of heart, of your spirit-energy, your life force. Throughout each day, try to remain positive no matter what chaos is around you. A positive outlook and attitude will give you continuous happiness boosts. Expect the best and work hard to always do your best. This is a tall order, but it is the only way to live at ten. We should try to give back more than we've been given, grateful for all that others have done for us and continue to do for us to sustain and help us maintain our life.

Value your childlike playfulness and sense of curiosity. To lighten up, brighten up. Laughter and humor help us keep our balance, our sense of proportion. Let life happen, enjoy the pleasures available in the moment, and value your own cheerfulness as you appreciate smiles and upbeat moods in others.

Contemplate life from the highest point of view. The change you want in others is likely the change you must make in yourself.

Happiness requires discipline, a striving to improve our habits of mind and spirit to live well and be of service to others. We will never become complacent when we live at ten because there is always more we can do to live with greater fulfillment and purpose. Live at ten and you will live with few regrets: This is how you share and spread happiness.

LIVE WITH NO TIME OUT.

Simone de Beauvoir

4

Pay Attention

HAPPINESS IS NOT SOMETHING
READY-MADE . . . IT COMES FROM
YOUR OWN ACTIONS.

The Dalai Lama

Awareness precedes happiness. So many people are spinning around so fast they're not present to experiences in front of their nose. Be aware of what's happening around you and inside you by learning to be consciously present in the wholeness of now. We must know, notice, and observe in order to achieve happiness for two. We should continuously strive to learn, and to know the reality of our true essence, of who we uniquely are.

One of the great aids to my intellectual and spiritual growth has been my ability to concentrate my mental powers on one object as a way to become more mindful. Every day I practice one-object meditation. I usually focus on a flower on my desk, first thing in the morning. Through the power of our attention, we can become one with a flower, a sunset, or a child's smile. When we pay attention, we observe with loving consideration. We practice being here, now, in unity with our breath and life.

As mindful lovers, we should try not to take each other for granted. Continuously remind yourself that you want to please each other. We should pay attention to the truth that we can never, ever change another person. We can be ourselves, we can encourage through example and discipline, but we shouldn't play the role of reformer. There is only one person on this planet we can improve. When we focus our attention inward, we can always better ourselves. Be responsible for your own life, and acknowledge the inevitable difficulties we all face.

Pay attention to your mood. If you are under stress, anxious, or out of sorts, be even more mindful. Are you conscious of your breathing? Are you aware of what you are feeling and thinking? Are you getting enough sleep? Are you spending enough time alone, together? Do you have enough free time? Are you always on the go? Do you feel overwhelmed? Do you have a tendency to complain that you're overworked? Are you rushing to catch up? Are you often impulsive and inattentive? Do you feel pressured? Are you becoming addicted to technology? Other people often pressure us to go to events they plan, and it's difficult to say no. Be alert to your need to make some changes in order to improve your situation. How can you eliminate unnecessary distractions? Do you often want just to be left alone?

Finding balance in our lives is not easy, but it is essential if we are on a quest to love one another more deeply and enjoy great and lasting happiness. We need to be aware of who we are and not let outside circumstances push us around.

If you love nature, but work in a room with no window, perhaps you can park your car several blocks from your office and walk on a tree-lined street, enjoying the fresh air. You can bring a plant to the office and hang a poster of a favorite garden painting by Impressionist Claude Monet.

Pay attention to what you do yourself and what you delegate. Emerson had this insight: "When I go into my garden with a spade, and dig a bed, I feel such exhilaration and health that I discover that I have been defrauding myself all this time in telling others to do for me what I should have done with my own hands."

Be aware of how you feel when you do various activities. Whenever you love what you're doing, you will be more lovable. By paying close attention to your needs and desires, you will live more vibrantly. Keep doing more and more things that bring you greater happiness. Take charge of your life on your own terms. Learn what works and what doesn't. Pay attention to all your actions, and let go of unnecessary things that weigh you down.

Everything we do lovingly can become a form of meditation when we train our mind and heart through paying attention.

CANNOT WE LET PEOPLE BE THEMSELVES,
AND ENJOY LIFE IN THEIR OWN WAY?

Emerson

Read Some Quality Literature Regularly

KNOWLEDGE IS
THE FOOD OF THE SOUL.

Plato

A love of learning is a gift that enriches every day we're alive. Reading quality literature regularly fosters within you a quickening of knowledge and experience. Eric Butterworth, a beloved spiritual teacher at The Unity Center in New York City, taught us that if you study one subject for one hour a day, seven days a week, twelve months a year, you can become an expert in five years.

The quality of our reading enhances all of our interactions with others and especially with our love. When you both value being lifelong students, always reaching out to grow more knowledgeable about the world and how to live more successfully in it, you become more interested and therefore more *interesting* to each other. Both partners raise their appreciation of life's richness and diversity and sustain a mutual joie de vivre. When you stimulate your mind with wise thoughts and universal principles that have withstood the test of time, you're more able to trust your intuition of what is true.

This commitment to the development of our mind throughout our lifetime is a noble enterprise. Sadly, in this age of technology, we are rushing to keep up. Reading great literature these days is often neglected.

Unless we put high value on this essential ingredient to personal happiness, we will be depriving ourselves of living well. Arthur Winter, a neurosurgeon, cautioned that "For your brain to thrive, it needs exercise, nourishment, and protection from toxins."

Reading imaginative, powerful writing exercises our brain. By turning off the "breaking news" on television, we can heighten our wisdom and feed our soul. The nineteenth-century English poet John Keats pointed out, "Nothing is finer for the purpose of great productions than a very gradual ripening of the intellectual powers."

A most specific quality of great literature is that it always demonstrates the undeniable will of humankind. We see our own possibilities and come to value our own potential. The mythology teacher Joseph Campbell urged us to "follow our bliss." He followed his by going away and reading for five years. "A hero," he taught, "is someone who has given his or her life to something bigger than oneself." Aristotle is a hero to me. As I read and reread his works, I have a deepened sense of my own worth as an individual. The fourteenth-century Italian poet Dante praised Aristotle as "the master of those who know."

The Modern Library Classics published *The Basic Works of Aristotle*, edited by Richard McKeon. They are, in his words, "an encyclopedic organization of human knowledge." This brilliant introduction into philosophy reveals the human soul as comprised of perception, imagination, movement, and reason. Aristotle knew that the highest human good is happiness, "an active life of the elements that has a rational principle." We are seeking health, wholeness, and what is good for us and others.

Studying the master teachers inspires us to do what we need to do and to pass on some of these universal truths to future generations.

Give yourself assignments. Have a reading list. Let one project lead to another. Once you develop this mutual habit, you will find learning to be a key to your shared happiness.

LEARNING IS A NAME SUPERIOR
TO BEAUTY; LEARNING IS BETTER
THAN HIDDEN TREASURE. LEARNING
IS A COMPANION ON A JOURNEY
TO A STRANGE COUNTRY; LEARNING
IS STRENGTH INEXHAUSTIBLE.

The Hitopadesa

6

Go on Vacations Alone, Together

BY AND LARGE, MOTHERS AND HOUSEWIVES ARE
THE ONLY WORKERS WHO DO NOT HAVE
REGULAR TIME OFF. THEY ARE
THE GREAT VACATIONLESS CLASS.

Anne Morrow Lindbergh

Peter and I spend our vacations very differently than most people we know. The American Heritage dictionary defines vacation as a period of time devoted to rest or relaxation from work or study. While we go on many short vacations, we've never wanted to devote time to rest or relaxation at the expense of work or study. In truth, we embrace the freedom to escape from our normal life in order to read, study, and write. I still remember writing in Paris on our honeymoon.

Anne Morrow Lindbergh, author of *Gift from the Sea*, tells us that women are the "great vacationless class." When Peter and I had children in the nest, we traveled together as a family. Now that our children are married and many of them have their own families, we don't take vacations together except on rare occasions. I remember going to Florida to an island with our two daughters and Alexandra's three small children as a gift for our thirtieth wedding anniversary. Alexandra and her husband rented a house on the beach. I assure you it was not an experience for Alexandra that was the classic definition of a vacation. It was happy and fun, but with three toddlers at the beach, it was nonstop work.

Even when we were raising our children, Peter and I made a special effort to take vacations with each other. When couples have all the responsibilities of family and work, it is *especially* important to go on vacations for two in order to keep the flame alive and become lovers again.

When lovers go on vacations with friends, there isn't the spontaneity to do whatever you wish to do. Even a few days away can bring partners closer together than ever. If you can't manage to go on a vacation alone, together, it would be better to bring the children than to leave them at home while you go off with friends. But with some careful planning and a meticulous rearranging of priorities, you can find a way to take a short vacation alone, together at least once a year.

Happiness for two requires nourishing each other in isolation where you don't see friends or family. Remember when you were first in love and how you always wanted to be alone together? Why? It's so marvelous, this relationship that is sparked with a touch of the divine, you can't let each other out of your sight. Then what happened? Why don't so many lovers still seek this privacy and intimacy and this wondrous sensuality?

When we go to Paris to celebrate our anniversary every May, we hang out in cafés, walk about the city, make no plans ahead of time for our meals, and experience the greatest happiness knowing a city we love so dearly is always there to help us celebrate our mutual love, year after year.

Vacations alone, together, are sacred. Each is a blessing and an opportunity to enjoy abundant happiness for two in an atmosphere that embraces your love.

THE GREAT ADVANTAGE OF A
HOTEL IS THAT IT'S A REFUGE
FROM HOME LIFE.

George Bernard Shaw

Assume More Responsibility at Home

A WOMAN SPENDS FIVE
TIMES MORE THAN A MAN ON WEEKLY
HOUSEHOLD TASKS.

**Agricultural Research
Service of U.S. Department of Agriculture**

C an we achieve the highest levels of individual happiness if we have too many domestic obligations?

Let us together think, think again, and rethink how we can assume more responsibilities at home to lighten the burden for our significant other. Men have come a long way to be more useful in the household, but they can become even more domestic.

Changing light bulbs, putting on a new roll of toilet paper, clearing the dinner dishes, for instance, should be an automatic desire once the need is there. If our partner doesn't notice a light bulb is burned out and needs to be replaced and doesn't know where the light bulbs are stored, his lover will have to do this chore or two people would live in darkness. It is thoughtful to go around with a garbage bag and empty the wastebaskets. If you get up after your partner, you should make the bed! When you genuinely want harmony at home, assume more responsibility. Men who are confident in their masculinity can show their love by taking on some things that were once thought to be the domain of women.

Both partners should know how the house works. When we share in the process of homemaking, neither partner carries too heavy a load. Let's end the division of labor at home! We'll build a better society with more lasting relationships when each of us willingly assumes more responsibility at home, doing more small and necessary things as labors of love. Inconvenient, unpleasant domestic tasks should be no one's exclusive job.

The mythology teacher Joseph Campbell wrote, "The first function of mythology is to sanctify the place you are in." Our home is sacred and should be inviolate, secure from negative energy. The love and warmth we mutually expend on our home make it a delight to live there.

I think there should be a willingness to do whatever it takes to make both people feel blessed at home. Take pride in your house. Strive for mutual domestic bliss.

When the French invite someone to their home, they use the phrase *chez moi*—translated literally as "with me"—to denote their home. Yes, home should reflect you—both of you! We need better communication about the division of labor at home. Discuss things that can make a difference, making plans together in sincere cooperation. With diplomacy, we are not critical, but share as best we can whatever tasks are at hand.

There is a rhythm to the dance of daily life together. Both of you know to fold and put away clean towels. Both load and unload the dishwasher. Both change the bed linens. Recycle together. Know where the tinfoil is, the dustpan, an apron, and garbage bags and learn how and be willing to do more and more things to be useful at home:

Know how to

- change a fuse
- turn off the water
- start the lawn mower

- tend the fire
- empty the garbage
- iron a shirt
- vacuum
- spackle, sand, and paint a room
- put up wallpaper
- dust
- set an attractive table
- scrub the bathtub
- tile a floor
- hang a shelf
- scrape, sand, and stain a floor
- serve breakfast in bed on a tray
- wax and polish tabletops
- arrange flowers
- unpack and put away the groceries
- clean the air-conditioner filters
- add to the grocery list

Don't wait to be asked. Show your love in action by seeing a need and doing your share. Rather than inquiring, "What's for dinner?" assume that you are making dinner. This is a true treat.

HE IS THE HAPPIEST, BE
HE KING OR PEASANT,
WHO FINDS PEACE IN HIS HOME.

Goethe

Have 50–50 Voting Power

LOVE WILL NEVER BE ANYWHERE
EXCEPT WHERE EQUALITY AND UNITY ARE.

Meister Eckhart

We share everything when we love each other. We should share our power to decide how to best find happiness for two. Try to make decisions together. Anything not mutual is most often not fair. Accepting equality is the only way not to have one person dominate the other. The more we have, the more we're able to share. 50–50 voting power is win-win. When there is mutual support and love, you can know the greatest happiness as you meet life's challenges. You have each other 100 percent. Fifty plus fifty equals 100 percent.

Equal power is not the same as equal distribution. If one person inherits money or property, it is theirs for the time being. If, however, a person shares the success with their partner, both are entitled to equal distribution.

We must power-share in order to act effectively in our relationship. We both benefit when we combine our intelligence, our experience, our resources, and our inspiration. We should communicate our own points of view about how we should spend our time, energy, and money. When we share the power equally, we tend to come to a consensus. When we agree, we both feel empowered.

Think of collaboration and compromise with your partner as the CC factor. We best work things out when we want the best for each other. We're far more powerful together than alone. When we share 50–50, it doesn't matter what the issue is, we want our partner to feel we've been fair and generous. Have you been equitable about your treatment of power in the past? Do you value your love's happiness as being as important as your own?

No one can take your share of power from you without your consent. Whether you're deciding where the children go to school, whether to move in order to accept a new job opportunity, or how to spend your vacation time, work things out together. The CC factor is an excellent technique for coming to an agreement lovingly. You have 50–50 voting power, but there are only two of you. The best way to break a stalemate is to be compassionate and keep in mind that your goal is to share a joyful life together while serving others. Common sense will guide you as you both elevate your potential to love, respect, and honor each other more deeply, sharing what you have, while exercising moral excellence.

BY THE JUST WE MEAN THAT
WHICH IS LAWFUL AND
THAT WHICH IS FAIR AND
EQUITABLE.

Aristotle

Criticize with Kindness

Two people who deeply love each other over a lifetime will encounter many situations where criticism is appropriate. However, no matter how well-meaning the criticism, it is always best to express your point of view kindly, with the goal of not hurting your partner's feelings. "Kindness," wrote Mark Twain, "is the language which the deaf can hear and the blind can see." When we are gentle, our partner senses our intention to help.

If we have an opinion about a course of action, any advice we offer may give the appearance of arrogance or insensitivity that can turn off the person on the receiving end. It is judicious to present your sound judgment in a loving manner. We can never be too kind when we are being honest. The wiser the advice, the greater the need to convey it in a generous, warmhearted way.

The more we practice the habit of speaking kindly, the better we can be understood. Remember also Benjamin Franklin's wise advice: "They that will not be counseled, cannot be helped."

It is best not to be a fault-finder with petty, nagging criticism. Some people are disposed to finding fault and they carp, complain, and quibble. Whenever two lovers get in the habit of beginning their criticism "you never" or "you always," it is not a good beginning.

I know that Peter would never intentionally try to hurt me, so whenever he does criticize me, I feel his respect. I want to learn, to stretch myself, to improve. Most of the time, I ask for his advice. We have to change and improve ourselves. A doctor told me years ago that no one can change another person more than 5 percent, and then there is the risk that the person will swing in the opposite direction.

It is wise not to cause unnecessary tension by picking at minor mistakes. If something is frustrating you—cat food in the kitchen sink or a toilet seat left up, wait until you are calm and centered to mention it. Think of all the compliments you have for your lover before you make a critical suggestion.

When we're kind, we're persuasive. As an interior designer I asked my clients to envision the big picture, not to dwell on the tiny details and minor flaws. In an intimate partnership, be high-hearted about what's really important: how blessed you are to love each other.

ADVICE IS SELDOM WELCOME;
AND THOSE WHO WANT IT
THE MOST ALWAYS LIKE IT
THE LEAST.

Lord Chesterfield

10

Encourage Each Other to Do Something Every Day That Will Boost Happiness

WHO IS THE HAPPIEST OF MAN?
HE WHO VALUES THE MERITS OF OTHERS AND IN THEIR
PLEASURE TAKES JOY, EVEN AS THOUGH IT WAS HIS OWN.

Goethe

I'm often asked at my happiness seminars whether one person can make another person happy. Yes and no. No one can make another person happy. Happiness is entirely up to the individual. But we all can be happier when we're with a happy person. Peter, for example, loves my cheerfulness. He's attracted to my energy, my spunk. He and I encourage each other to do something every day that will boost happiness. The great wisdom of this habit is that it works every time.

In order to increase your own happiness, you have to get into the happiness habit. I wrote about this in *Choosing Happiness*. Make a list of all the things that boost your happiness. Add to the list as you're reminded of other things you love to do that make you happier. Have your partner make a list. Share your lists with each other. Once a day, treat yourself to pursuing something for your own sake as well as taking the other person's happiness seriously. When two independent people are mutually happy, both of your lives are deeply enriched. Ideally there should be a parallel happiness where you are both equally thriving in a supportive environment.

Each day will have its own weather and emotions. Your lists will help remind you what could hit the happiness spot for you and your partner on a given day. After approximately three months you will experience a remarkable boost in your moods and attitudes. Keep encouraging each other to do something that boosts happiness every single day you are alive. This is a sure way to show your love for each other. Your list could include:

- playing tennis
- taking a yoga class
- going to a museum
- browsing at a bookstore
- going out to breakfast together
- going to the gym
- having your hair done or cut
- going to a café to read and sip espresso
- buying fresh flowers
- treating yourself to fresh berries for breakfast
- visiting the grandchildren
- taking a dance class
- writing a friend a letter
- taking a quilting class

Your partner's list could include:

- watching a funny movie
- going to a used-book store and getting lost in the stacks
- going swimming
- meeting a friend for a beer or a glass of wine after work
- playing the guitar
- dabbling in watercolors

- doing some woodworking
- baking brownies
- going for an afternoon walk with the dog
- writing poetry
- becoming absorbed in great music
- planning a vacation
- planting tulip bulbs
- wandering around the Container Store
- having a massage
- visiting your daughter over tea
- going to a lecture
- meeting a favorite author at a bookstore signing
- going for a sail
- flying a kite with a grandchild
- riding a bike
- going out to lunch together
- walking on the beach
- stargazing
- calling a friend who lives out of town
- painting a table blue
- writing in a journal
- taking pictures of your children

Our pleasures don't have to be complicated or expensive. A karate master instructs his pupils to seek happiness in the present and they'll find it in the future. Share with joy in each other's pursuits of happiness.

HE THAT DOES GOOD TO ANOTHER,
DOES GOOD ALSO TO HIMSELF.

Seneca

11

No Awkward Surprises

NO ONE DESIRES WHAT
IS UNKNOWN.

Ovid

Be careful about surprising your mate. Surprises can be awkward, catching us off guard. They don't allow us the natural good feelings we experience when we're free to anticipate something wonderful. I remember my mother gave me an unfortunate surprise party on my eighth birthday. She was so uptight about making it a surprise that she forgot to wish me a happy birthday that morning and didn't give me a card or present because they were meant to be "surprises" at the surprise party!

Grown-up surprises can backfire, too. No one can pack our suitcase for us, knowing what we want or need. If your lover is taking you to Tuscany for your twenty-fifth anniversary, you shouldn't be the last person to hear about it. Who knows—if asked, you might prefer to go to Provence.

The one who plans the surprise seems to me to be the controlling person in the process. Their partner may not be thrilled to be ambushed. Family, friends, and lovers are well-meaning when they plan to surprise their loved one, but it might be more thoughtful and loving to ask what would make the other person happiest. A surprise implies that someone

27

else is paying for the event, but even among lovers it is impossible to clearly read such situations. Isn't it better to ask first? The one doing the surprising might feel confident he or she is doing something quite wonderful, when, in fact, it could be a sly way of doing what is not mutually enjoyable. Not everyone wants to go on a cruise ship or go to Europe with their in-laws or have a surprise birthday party given for them when the friends invited were not the ones they want to be with on this sentimental day.

Instead of assuming something is terrific, I prefer to have a discussion. If Peter wants to do something for me, he'll invite me to dinner and then ask me where I'd like to go. He'll promise me theater tickets and I'm able to select the play. He'll buy me a new pen and we go together to select the one that "speaks" to me.

Of course, "little" surprises you know your love will adore are always welcome. I call these "ninis":

- bring favorite flowers home
- buy a bottle of wine for dinner
- select a pastry for breakfast
- pick up a new book by a favorite author
- bring home a copy of a news magazine
- give a small box of Godiva chocolate truffles

When I turned sixty-five last year I didn't want any presents, but I wanted Peter's presence at fun events. Peter made a huge fuss over me and let me feel loved and adored as we planned sweet romantic adventures. We ended up in Barbados for a week where we both wrote each morning for five hours on a terrace that faced the ocean waves. We were alone, together, both doing what we wanted to do. Best of all: no awkward surprises. The entire vacation I was surprised by joy. I brought all the books I wanted to read, my writing materials, my favorite resort clothes, and we shared a private, intimate experience as a result of our planning to escape alone together.

Be wise. Be glad you asked.

GIVING PRESENTS IS A TALENT,
TO KNOW WHAT A PERSON WANTS,
TO KNOW WHEN AND HOW TO GET IT,
TO GIVE IT LOVINGLY AND WELL.

Pamela Glenconner

Together, Explore Your Spirituality

MAN'S PERFECTION WOULD BE THE
FULFILLMENT OF HIS END; AND HIS
END WOULD BE UNION WITH HIS MAKER.

William James

I vividly remember a phone conversation years ago with a good friend who paused and exclaimed, as if she'd had a sudden revelation, "Alexandra, your books are really spiritual." I laughed. I'd never thought about my books being particularly spiritual. As an interior designer I've written a great deal about our physical, tangible environment, not necessarily about the immaterial soul-world within.

Over the years, though, my writing has become more philosophical. I am, indeed, a lover of wisdom and try to take a calm and rational approach toward life. Ever since 1959 when I traveled around the world I've studied spirituality from a global perspective along with ancient Greek philosophy.

Because of my exposure to so many different cultures and beliefs at an impressionable age, I've made it a habit to study world religions and absorb as much truth as possible, resulting, I think, in greater insights. All religions seem to hold up love as the ideal. We must constantly discipline our minds to consider and practice the goodness that is taught by spiritual leaders. We need to strengthen our inner resources as we develop a kinder, more loving, compassionate heart.

It is desirable and pleasant to mutually explore spirituality. When a couple spends time and effort exploring these thoughts and feelings, they will be making formidable mutual ties.

As we explore together ways to increase our happiness, we should make a point of encouraging each other to practice this discipline daily. Through reading, going to services, retreats, lectures, meditation, and prayer, we will gain greater happiness and experience less suffering. We come to understand firsthand the true meaning of unity, of connecting, of love in the service of others. We acquire in this way personal spiritual authority by contemplating love in its limitless power. By training our mind and cultivating the deepest inner values a human being can live by, we're able to embrace love, happiness, and inner peace.

Explore spiritual variety. Become more receptive to other ways of finding inner clarity and transformation. Be willing to let go of some of the teachings that you have outgrown because now you may believe them to be less compelling truths. Dare to explore the mystery from a broader perspective. Through studying different points of view, you can think for yourself, maintaining an open mind.

Ask each other questions. Encourage thoughtful communication. Expand on these questions exploring the mysteries of spirituality. The French philosopher Albert Schweitzer, who believed in reverence for life, understood that "sincerity is the foundation of the spiritual life." As lovers, you are in a nonthreatening environment. Together you both can discuss intelligent design, evolution, reincarnation, life after death. Do you believe in divine grace? Do you believe in miracles? Do you believe in angels? Be each other's spirit guides. Don't ever feel satisfied you have discovered the ultimate truth. Continue on your quest. When we heard that the Vietnamese Buddhist monk Thich Nhat Hanh was leading a conference in Amherst, Massachusetts, Peter and I took a train to be present for his teachings. We did the same when His Holiness the Dalai Lama came to New York City.

Saint Teresa of Avila understood: "Even the sun and stars borrow light from the light of consciousness. The Self shining." In his brilliant psychological study *The Varieties of Religious Experience* published in 1902, psychologist and philosopher William James noted, "An idea, to be suggestive, must come to the individual with the force of revelation." Through mutual study and practice, many wise truths will be revealed to us. I believe we have a responsibility to deepen our love and compassion for our human family, who deserve to be happy and live in peace, and this process begins at home.

THE HIGHEST INSIGHT A MAN
CAN ATTAIN IS THE YEARNING
FOR PEACE, FOR THE UNION
OF HIS WILL WITH AN INFINITE WILL.

Albert Schweitzer

13

Write Each Other's New Year's Resolutions

THE GREATEST GOOD YOU CAN DO
FOR ANOTHER IS NOT JUST TO
SHARE YOUR RICHES, BUT TO REVEAL
TO HIM HIS OWN.

Benjamin Disraeli

The greatest way of showing our love is to recognize our lover's needs and riches and help him reveal and pursue his own. The Roman philosopher and emperor Marcus Aurelius understood human nature well: "A wrongdoer is often a man who has left some thing undone, not always one who has done something."

Our partner can help us with our resolutions to do the things we ought to do as well as the things we want to do. One lovely way to help each other in this ongoing process is to write each other's New Year's resolutions. The sweetest way to do this is to enter into a dialogue, with each of you taking notes. When we clearly see what our lover wants to do, we're in a position to help the other person see his potential better. When we know what someone wants and we wish it for him, our encouragement and support will be instrumental in their resolve to live up to their highest power.

There shouldn't be any secrets in this project. Nor is it meant to be a makeover to shape up our mate. Rather, I see this process as a way to show our love in action. Whether someone is struggling in a job he doesn't enjoy or wants to go to graduate school, we can be useful in helping our partner to make these changes. Over the years you will both be able to help each other to find greater enjoyment in all things you want to do.

In January 2007, my book *You Are Your Choices: 50 Ways to Live the Good Life* was published. At the beginning of the book, I invited the reader to go on a quest to live the good life: the life that is good for us, that feels right, and that is good for others. With that goal in mind, Peter and I made each other's New Year's resolutions.

Alexandra's Resolutions for Peter

- Keep up with your personal correspondence, as Abraham Lincoln so wisely recommended.
- Balance your checkbook—every check.
- Keep in better touch with your family.
- Be mindful of your posture every day.
- Walk more.
- Drink more water.
- Keep up with your filing and updating personal documents.
- Plan some great adventures.
- Read those classic books you've been putting off reading.
- Finish writing your book *Figure It Out* this year.
- Make vacation plans a year in advance.
- Go to bed earlier, get up earlier.
- Map out more time for contemplation.
- Learn to let go of past attachments.
- Thank more people for their personal kindnesses.
- Take better care of your finances.
- Write an up-to-date draft of your obituary.

- Recognize that self-improvement is an ongoing process that goes on every day of your life.

Peter's Resolutions for Alexandra

- Take more time for yourself to do whatever is pleasant for you at the moment.
- Go through all your clothes, shoes, and equipment and eliminate as much as you can: Others will benefit when you give things to family and donate to a thrift shop.
- Find out where you can dispose of valuable things you no longer want or need.
- Make inquiries about sunny places you wish to visit on winter vacations and find out what and where will make you happy.
- Resolve to develop a record of people's addresses and information: Your Filofax is a work in progress, but you must keep at it until you've fulfilled your resolution.
- Plan some parties that we will have outside our home on an intimate scale.
- When you're alerted, anywhere on the globe, of some event that is particularly compelling to you, we will be participants.
- Develop an exercise plan for the seasons of the year, giving yourself sufficient exercise that is healthy, appropriate, and enjoyable.
- Concentrate on learning as much as you can about preserving and enlarging your finances.
- Take better care of yourself day to day: avoid the nurse syndrome where you only take care of others; now focus this skill on yourself.

- Deal more effectively with the daily influx of mail and information in order to handle the flow: Keep up!
- Continue to always have flowers no matter what the circumstances, because I believe that is what makes you the happiest.
- Shoulders back: Stand up straight.
- Continue to take meticulous care of your clothes because they'll last and will always have style.
- Make more time regularly to plan to do certain things important to you: Keep writing, lecturing, and giving.

Resolve and re-resolve to live the good life that will bring you abundant happiness for two!

THE HIGHEST SERVICE WE CAN
PERFORM FOR OTHERS IS TO HELP
THEM HELP THEMSELVES.

Horace Mann

Celebrate More

Celebrations don't have to be large or expensive. Some of the happiest times Peter and I have together are little moments when we celebrate happiness for two. In my book *Living a Beautiful Life*, I wrote about the small but significant celebrations, ceremonies, and rituals we can perform at home to enrich our love of life.

All too often people get caught up in the anxiety of their fast-paced lives, feeling there is no time to celebrate. I feel we impoverish our spirit if we don't regularly come together for some planned happiness to make memorable moments beautiful.

Friends of ours have "demi-tasse" Sunday nights. After supper, Barbara and Garry each savor a scoop of low-fat vanilla ice cream drizzled with a demi-tasse spoonful (or two) of their son-in-law's hot chocolate sauce. This treat is a ritual they look forward to. They celebrate the coming week in a festive mood.

Other friends, Clyda and George, have Friday night supper by a cozy warm fire in the winter months. They look forward to being alone, together, for this date. Just the fact that they're dining in a different place makes it more celebratory, but the fire's charm also makes an ordinary evening a romantic one augmented by candles and flowers. The evening's conversation is elevated by the atmosphere.

Many people are good at entertaining others and will go to great lengths to attend to the details. Why isn't it even more important to go to a little extra effort to create these wonderful moments when you're alone, together? When I do something that increases our happiness, it gives me a burst of energy rather than exhausting me. Going the extra mile to create a pleasant experience is self-fulfilling. Pretend you're having two couples over for dinner. Plan the menu, what flowers you want, and all the details of setting the table. Then change your mind and postpone the dinner party and have the same details for you two only.

Having a friend over should be as simple as adding a chair and a place setting to the table, provided you two are already planning to celebrate. I don't believe we should do things for friends that we deprive ourselves of on a regular basis. The mere fact that we are alive is cause for celebration. Privately we're able to recognize and praise each other for no particular reason other than that we want to express our mutual love.

People ask me whether anyone is capable of being happy all the time. Unfortunately, the answer is no. However, I believe that through rigorous mind training, through meditation and greater understanding, we can eliminate unnecessary suffering through our awareness of what makes us and others happy.

Celebrations are not just to provide pleasure. They help us to honor each other, to recognize that, in truth, we should celebrate life together every day, wherever we are, right here, right now. When we say, "Let's celebrate," we are sending positive signals in all directions. Whether you arrange a tea tray ahead of time in order to have a tea celebration ready, or you set a pretty table for breakfast, you are elevating the ordinary with focused attention and sensuous awakening.

Someone who celebrates more lives more fully and loves more deeply. Illuminate your love. Sing praises. Together, celebrate each other.

COME TO ME . . . AND LET US
BE AS HAPPY AS WE CAN.

Samuel Johnson

Work Daily on Your Character

A MAN'S CHARACTER IS HIS FATE.

Heraclitus

What is more important than your character? Character is, after all, the badge of our fate. The ancient Chinese philosopher Confucius believed that "good and evil do not befall men without reason. Heaven sends them happiness or misery according to their conduct." Your character encompasses your moral and ethical strength. In order to love you have to feel you have love to give, and you won't have that unless you are on reasonably good terms with yourself. Anything that improves your character is more than a step in the right direction.

What are your distinguishing attributes? What is most typical of your behavior? What is your reputation? Are you held in high esteem? Do you have a clear conscience? What are some of your greatest character strengths, and what are some of your weaknesses you want to work on to improve?

Aristotle taught us that in order to live the good life, we have to act virtuously. Happiness, this wise philosopher understood, is "active virtue" and "moral excellence." When we are trying hard to love each other more purely, get along better, and be happier together, we should discipline ourselves to shine a bright light on our own behavior. What are the guiding principles of right conduct you value and want to live by?

As Peter and I traveled around the country on our last book tour, I inquired what people most admire in other people's character or in their own, and what the most important character traits were in a human being. I kept a notebook of the answers I received from readers. I collected over two thousand answers. All of them are valuable for us to live by. I was happily surprised to discover that generally people dwelled on the most challenging virtues. When we work daily on our own character, we discipline ourselves to live in keeping with these transcendent qualities.

Below, in their own words, are the virtues people cited, listed in order of frequency.

1. honesty
2. integrity
3. loyalty
4. compassion
5. empathy
6. kindness
7. humor
8. laughter
9. generosity ("a giving heart: bigheartedness")
10. patience
11. joy ("ability to maintain joy")
12. gratitude
13. positive outlook/attitude
14. openness
15. love (not as high on the list as I would have expected!)
16. happiness (not as high on the list as I would have thought)
17. curiosity

18. strength
19. fairness
20. courage
21. bravery
22. nobility
23. resilience
24. altruism
25. cheerfulness
26. understanding
27. spirit
28. independence
29. optimism
30. authenticity ("Be true to yourself without fear or pretense." "Let go of the mask." "Show up." "Give eye contact.")
31. acceptance ("allowing other people to be who they are")
32. hardworking
33. inner peace (calmness)
34. competence
35. virtue
36. giving
37. dependability
38. people of substance
39. aging gracefully ("women who are not trying to hold their place in time")
40. consistency of character
41. unselfishness
42. being present ("They are in the moment." "They contact your spirit.")
43. a gentle spirit
44. risk taker

45. creativity
46. childlike curiosity
47. encourager (and wanting others to be encouragers)
48. perseverance
49. friendship
50. unconditional friendship
51. genuine ("Really real person. Be who you are and be good at it. Be at ease with who you are.")
52. passionate
53. contentment
54. ability to find peace
55. reputation
56. straightforward (candid, direct, plain-talking)
57. strong opinions
58. driven
59. nourishing
60. spontaneity
61. conscientious
62. steady
63. intelligence
64. friendly
65. willingness to stick with your convictions
66. smiles
67. good listener (a listening ear)
68. energy
69. self-confidence
70. outgoing
71. openness
72. fire in the soul
73. dignity

74. upbeat nature
75. idealism
76. faith
77. sincerity
78. tolerance
79. enthusiasm
80. people who walk the walk, not talk the talk (people whose path is their example, not their word)
81. joie de vivre
82. ability to step back and appreciate the moment you're in
83. colorful
84. tell the hard truth lovingly
85. order
86. simplicity
87. intuition
88. sense of wonder
89. peacefulness
90. competitive
91. "Be the everyday person. Keep going."
92. daring
93. meet new people
94. stay in touch with friends
95. fun-loving ("people who get the most enjoyment from life")
96. being a perpetual student
97. love of life
98. forgiveness
99. punctuality
100. humility
101. reliability
102. fortitude ("No matter what you're presented with")

103. "Do it today"
104. being real
105. charity ("When you give, it comes back to you fully." "In giving you receive, because charity is full of love.")
106. give pleasure in visual things ("Food and flowers create happiness.")
107. versatility
108. articulate
109. sense of willingness
110. modesty
111. honor
112. hopeful
113. service
114. reverence
115. humility
116. nurturing
117. charm
118. consciousness
119. inventiveness

From my research, honesty is far and away the characteristic people most admire in others as well as in themselves.

What do you most admire in another's character? What do you value in your own character? I think my main character trait is "perseverance," although the two traits I most admire in others are love and happiness. I'm tenacious. I persevere and persist and have a tendency to remain constant to a purpose in spite of obstacles. I try to turn problems into situations, setbacks, challenges. Aristotle warned us that character building is difficult, that wrong behavior is easy. Sheila, an attractive young mother of two daughters, told me her favorite saying:

"If only we tried as hard to be good as we try to be beautiful." In Sheila's grandmother's high school yearbook, the caption under her picture was "as kind as she is fair."

Whenever I am challenged by life's curveballs, I know I have more work to do on my character. We all have work to do. Every day we can discipline ourselves to select one of the listed virtues and work on it for a day. We build our character by thought, word, and action, habit by habit, revealing our moral purpose, assuming our duty faithfully. Good habits strengthen our goodness. This is the one true way to live a life of honor, integrity, and dignity. Virtue attracts virtue.

The cancer doctor Bernie Siegel tells us that "When you do the work necessary to clear your conscience, then the joy of living returns and the physiology of optimism restores you." I asked Peter what he admires most in people's character, and he wrote this list:

- Keep your word.
- Discipline your habits.
- Be grateful, gracious, and kind.
- Share and give credit to others.
- Be generous.
- Be forgiving and understanding.
- Recognize love as life's exquisite mystery.

Years ago I read the wise words of a first-century B.C. Roman poet, Marial, that fit Peter well: "Virtue extends our days. He lives two lives who relives his past with pleasure."

We honor our self when we follow through on honest acts and principles. By daily working on our own character, we find less pain in the discipline and take more pleasure in active virtue and moral excellence: the keys to our own happiness, extended to others.

Although no human being can make another person happy, happiness can be contagious. The same principle applies to character. We greatly influence others by our own continuous practice of virtue. Through example, encouragement, and support, we help others near and far. Our greatest resource is our goodness. Trust yourself in your own pursuit of good character, and noble people will be attracted to you.

MAN SCANS WITH SCRUPULOUS CARE
THE CHARACTER AND PEDIGREE OF
HIS HORSES, CATTLE, AND DOGS BEFORE
HE MATCHES THEM; BUT WHEN
HE COMES TO HIS OWN MARRIAGE
HE RARELY, OR NEVER, TAKES ANY
SUCH CARE.

Charles Darwin

16

Begin Each Encounter with a Smile

A GENUINE SMILE GIVES US
HOPE, FRESHNESS.

The Dalai Lama

A genuine smile warms hearts, and it is true that when you smile, the whole world smiles with you. Last year, in Memphis, I was at a Starbucks waiting to go on a live morning news television show when two clowns appeared. Jewels and Jingles were also scheduled to appear on the television show, to promote the circus coming to town. Jewels and Jingles both said that the best thing they've ever done was to be clowns with balloons, funny sounds, and smiling children.

Jingles tells his own children that they're wasting their energy frowning. It's easier to smile. It takes more muscles to frown, to wrinkle the brow. A frown is literally a downer, dampening our spirit, depressing our mood. A smile indicates pleasure, affection, amusement, recognition, and approval. Happiness research suggests that people smile in the mirror when they are at the bathroom sink because the smile will communicate positively to our brain and cells. "Wrinkles," suggests Mark Twain, "should merely indicate where smiles have been."

Several years ago, Peter and I had the privilege of hearing the teachings of His Holiness the Dalai Lama when he was in New York City. For three and a half days, we were in his presence a few feet from the stage, experiencing the pure, luminous energy of this holy man. The Dalai Lama's smile is contagious. He has a twinkle that speaks volumes of his elevated and joyful consciousness.

Just as you don't need any reason to be happy, you don't need any particular circumstance to decide to smile. Be mindful of the power of your smile to increase happiness—yours and others'. The nineteenth-century English writer William Makepeace Thackeray told us, "The world is a looking glass and gives back to every man the reflection of his own face. Frown at it and it will in turn look sourly upon you; laugh at it and with it, and it is a jolly, kind companion."

A smile is a gift we freely give. If people are grateful, they will return the smile. Begin each encounter with the affirmation of a smile. It is a wonderful way to make friends. We appear open, receptive, and ready to connect. A smile has the opposite energy of a clenched fist.

The Dalai Lama reminds us that "we are all human beings. We all have the capacity to relate to one another with warmth, with affection, with friendship." A smile shows a generosity of spirit. Give the gift of your radiant smile and keep in mind that love is never inappropriate. Don't smile with the need to have someone smile back at you. Smile because it brings sunshine to others as well as to you.

Think of the Zen proverb that teaches us that we are two mirrors facing each other and there is no image in between. Our tender feelings toward our loved one are reinforced through a sweet look that makes our heart melt with a smile. Awaken to a new day smiling as you say your mantra and meditate about the blessings of a new day in love. When you are in the habit of smiling as you awaken, you then share the morning smile with your love. When your partner enters a room, look up from your book or newspaper and smile. When you arrive home from work, don't say hi while putting down your briefcase, mail, and groceries. Rather than having your head down and your back turned, take an extra two seconds and smile at your loved one. Smiles lead to kisses.

There are no words to express just how much we mean to each other. A smile is nonverbal communication that speaks volumes.

OUR REAL PERSONALITY IS
ALL LIGHT, ALL LOVE, ALWAYS
SHINING.

Upanishads

17

Don't Let Children Control You

AT EVERY STEP THE CHILD SHOULD
BE ALLOWED TO MEET THE REAL
EXPERIENCES OF LIFE;
THE THORNS SHOULD NEVER BE
PLUCKED FROM HIS ROSES.

Ellen Kay

If you are a parent, you may be more than aware that children can be manipulative. If you have stepchildren, this can further complicate the situation. When a child tries to control you, it is inappropriate. Children may attempt to take over and feel entitled, especially in matters that directly affect them, but remember that you and your partner are in charge of how you live your life.

Parents who are worried that they'll feel lonely when their youngest child leaves the nest can relax. Studies prove that their "happiness for two" dips considerably when their first child is born and doesn't spike until they have an empty nest. What was all about the children can now be all about you. You'll have newfound freedom to come and go as you please, going along on your partner's business trips or simply enjoying more sensual privacy at home. If you overcontrol your children, this is an invitation to let them control you. Everything goes both ways.

Keep in mind that your children are young men and women of the universe. They are not yours. You have the temporary responsibility to care for them until they leave home. After a child is approximately twenty-one years old, you should let your daughter or son fly. Let the universe teach them what further they need to know. Don't clip their wings with your opinions. Unsolicited advice is rarely welcome. Be grateful they are independent and able to take care of themselves without your monetary support. Love never pressures.

If you genuinely wish nothing but happiness for your children, take care of your happiness for two and don't look back. If you are thriving, you won't be a burden to your children and they will not have any reason to try to control you unless for purely selfish reasons. They won't feel responsible for you and worried about how you manage life's changing chapters as you grow older if you are doing a good job managing your own affairs. Be grateful that your child loves and honors you and wants you to be happy. Don't ask for too much advice.

When parents can't let go of their grown children, it limits the lives of all concerned. Adult children lose confidence in their own powers. Be busy making your own plans. Let your children make their own mistakes and correct them, without your help. They're going to do whatever they want to do, anyway. They're now able to drive, vote, and pay taxes. By showing support and being interested in their independence, we help them grow from dependency to freedom.

We're given approximately eighteen years to love our children as children, care for their basic needs, raise them in a happy, supportive environment, encourage their desires, and shape their character. This intensively focused time when they are at home and in school is the only time we are in some control of our children. Once they leave home, they come back for short visits as guests. Maintain your happiness together throughout this evolving process, because it is natural for them to leave you.

With luck, you'll have the gift of grandchildren—the sublime blessing our children bring to us.

MEN DO NOT THINK
OF SONS AND DAUGHTERS,
WHEN THEY FALL IN LOVE.

Elizabeth Barrett Browning

Listen With a Third Ear

IT TAKES TWO TO SPEAK THE TRUTH—
ONE TO SPEAK, AND ANOTHER TO HEAR.

Henry David Thoreau

There is an art and talent to deep listening. Whenever we're talking, we're not learning anything new. Approximately 95 percent of the thoughts we have today are carryovers from yesterday and the days before. When we listen with love, we listen with a third ear. Our soul is present when we listen undividedly.

When I am focused, one-on-one in conversation, I'm offended if the other person tunes out and stops listening. Because I like to be heard when I speak, I'm sensitive to others who are talking and I try to concentrate on what they are saying.

Sometimes people don't tell you everything. If your partner mentions a movie that sounds interesting, you can listen intuitively and may see that this is something you should do together, something good to share, even if this was not suggested. You can see into a comment when you listen with a third ear.

When we deeply listen, we pay attention to the other person's body language, especially the facial expression, the selection of words, and the voice intonation. All give us clues to the full message. From this awareness, we can tell whether the other person is happy or unhappy with the current situation.

Listening requires an open heart, a vulnerability and receptivity. We only hear what we're capable of receiving. If we're not receptive, we don't hear.

Dr. Bernie Siegel advises us to show up and listen. "Don't ever forget the power of listening and the strength it takes just to be there—not curing, but caring." The world is in need of listeners.

Just as there is an art to listening, so there is an art of questioning in order to open the other person to tell their innermost truths. One of Dr. Siegel's young patients who came to work as a paid intern at my interior design firm in the late eighties was an amazing listener. She was like a sponge, absorbing information and inspiration. Claire asked intelligent questions and then listened. I knew Claire was dying at the time I hired her. While visiting her at Sloan-Kettering Cancer Center in New York three months after she came to work with me, just days before she died, I asked her a question. "What can I do for you?" With an inquiring and sad expression, she looked up at me from her bed, and then said, with some humor, "Alexandra, you can give me a new body."

Try not to ask a question that can be answered as though it were a true-or-false test, or with a yes or no. Rather than asking, "Did you have a good day?" ask, "What was the most interesting thing that happened to you today?" Peter had a legal assistant who was brilliant but painfully shy and socially awkward. If I asked Ralph any question that could possibly be answered with yes or no I'd hear back "yes, ma'am" or "no, ma'am." I learned not to ask, "Are you enjoying the challenges of this trial?" but would inquire, "What are the most challenging things about the trial?"

The author Edith Wharton claimed that she knew how to listen when clever men were talking. "That is the secret of what you call my influence." One of the major men she listened to was the writer and critic Henry James. Henry's brother, the psychologist and philosopher William James, knew that "the first thing to learn in intercourse with others is noninterference with their own peculiar ways of being happy, provided these ways do not interfere with yours."

We should listen to everyone and not always be the speaker. Sometimes I regret that I have done too much of the talking. The Japanese close their eyes in order to listen better, to hear the truth. Humble, quiet people are usually wise and understand how to listen with a third ear. Some people are tuned in to others' mental vibrations and can get on the same wavelength without words being expressed. Even when we express strong differences of opinion, the writer Goethe believed "we can make of this earth a garden."

Listening is the first gift of communication. Listening with love will make our conversations persuasive and vividly enjoyable.

EVERY HUMAN BEING HAS A GREAT
YET OFTEN UNKNOWN GIFT TO CARE,
TO BE COMPASSIONATE, TO BE PRESENT
TO THE OTHER, TO LISTEN, TO HEAR, AND
TO RECEIVE. IF THAT GIFT WOULD BE SET
FREE AND MADE AVAILABLE,
MIRACLES COULD TAKE PLACE.

Henri J. Nouwen

19

It's Okay to Agree to Disagree

GRACE UNDER PRESSURE.

Ernest Hemingway

'm not certain opposites attract. Life is complex enough without having the one you love the most have a quite different perspective on life, a wholly different point of view. Hearing opposite opinions is stimulating and I enjoy the vital conversations when we both express our feelings and thoughts. When we basically concur with each other's universal principles, our talks seem to increase domestic harmony, but it is stimulating to have a different worldview and to be able to listen and learn from each other in a loving atmosphere. Agreeing to disagree is a useful diplomatic means of sharing different points of view amicably.

Happiness for two increases when we love each other just as we are. In my book *Things I Want My Daughters to Know*, one of my essays was entitled, "No One Will Ever Understand You." Although we seem to have a deep craving to be understood, wanting someone to grasp our essential nature, no other human will ever entirely comprehend our complex emotions. We all have our own mysterious nature that no one can access fully. Our job is to be mindful of ourselves and to be as understanding as possible about our soul mate and our differences. With patience and an open heart, we can come to see that we share more values than discord.

Not agreeing is no reason to become disagreeable. I don't appreciate people who try to brainwash me into going along with their opinion when I find their political or religious beliefs incompatible with mine. Some people feel they're dead right, when I may feel they are dead wrong. We all must exercise tolerance. Voltaire confounded his enemies when he insisted, "I disapprove of what you say, but I will defend to the death your right to say it."

Some people can be frightening in their intransigence. Whenever you air an opposing point of view, they get visibly upset and won't continue the conversation. You're reduced to changing the subject or remaining silent because so many topics are off limits. How can love grow in such a climate? Thomas Jefferson was so frustrated by this intolerance that he would plead, "For God's sake, let us freely hear both sides."

When we focus on our happiness for two, we come to understand that we can agree to disagree in harmony where we're able to express ourselves openly in a supportive atmosphere.

When I was a child, I tended to think that whatever I was taught, read, or told by my parents was the ultimate truth. We grow up to realize this is not true. Cicero reminds us not to be gullible: "One doesn't have to believe everything one hears."

Whatever our opinions about philosophy, religion, politics, morality, parenting, and social issues, I'd like to think we're capable of evolving to embrace unity. Couples may come to a point of disagreement and have tested it long and wide. That is when they recognize they're not going to be unified on that major issue. We can agree to disagree and have the courage to reconsider our views through study, meditation and, of course, changing circumstances.

WE MUST NOT CONFUSE DISSENT
WITH DISLOYALTY.

Edward R. Murrow

20

Nurture Your Core Identity

THERE IS VERY LITTLE DIFFERENCE
BETWEEN ONE MAN AND ANOTHER,
BUT WHAT LITTLE THERE IS,
IS VERY IMPORTANT.

William James

Who are you? What is the DNA of your soul? What characteristics are definitively "you"? At your center, your innermost vital part, what is most important? Tell me of your substance, the intangible qualities that are true to you.

Each of us should nurture our core identity by doing things that help us to become the person we really are and want to become. Through this commitment to know the heart of what really matters to us, we can grow in self-confidence, understanding we are on our path and headed in the right direction to express our unique and fullest human potential.

The process of self-knowing occurs largely by instinct and intuition. When we are calm and quiet, we become more attuned to these inner promptings. Erich Fromm taught us in *The Art of Loving* that "Only the person who has faith in himself is able to be faithful to others." Self-love is the start of loving others. First things first. The Buddha told us to "make of yourself a light."

Tending our inner patterns of behavior, nurturing our natural capabilities and aptitudes guides our hearts toward benevolence. Consciously we must focus our attention on the concrete things that burnish our unique aptitude and skills. If you love to sketch you might become an artist or designer. If you are a natural storyteller, you might become a fiction writer. If you love animals, you might choose to become a veterinarian. If you're a natural good cook, maybe you want to become a chef. Or, maybe you want to become a teacher, a quick way to learning yourself. Whatever we do to improve our innate talents can always benefit others as we fulfill ourselves through volunteering at the animal shelter, or being a literacy volunteer. If you are an artist you can go regularly to a hospice group and draw pictures for the patients or go once a week to help out at a church homeless shelter.

What are you meant to do with this mysterious privilege of being human? What can you bring out from the center of your soul and share with others? What do you need in order to grow more deeply? Make a list of some specific things you need to do to improve yourself:

- Consciously develop a better vocabulary. Whenever you come across a word that is unfamiliar to you, look it up in the dictionary, write down the meaning, then try to use the word in general communication.
- Build time into your daily schedule to paint.
- Spend twenty minutes alone each day.
- Take a class to learn a new hobby.
- Buy books you can study and mark to improve your skills in particular areas of interest.
- To improve your vitality, walk at least a half hour a day.
- Spend more time photographing the beauty of nature.
- Bring your sketchpad with you to record great architectural details.

What sacrifices are you willing to make to live the artistic spirit? Men and women who are brave and nurture their core identity are capable of doing great things with their lives when they have this unwavering commitment to try to use all their powers. When we accept this challenge and tenaciously follow our own path, we feel a sense of equality with others where we connect soul to soul, center to center, heart to heart, essence to essence, happiness to happiness, love to love.

As a woman, wife, homemaker, mother, grandmother, interior designer, writer, and lecturer, I'm aware every day how vitally important it is for me to nurture my essence and to balance the different areas of my being that are of great importance to me. I try to pay careful attention to what's most important to me at the time. Priorities change instantaneously. Sometimes I'm not needed by others and I use the time to study and do my inner work. But no matter how many demands on my time, energy, and money, I'm aware of an essential key to happiness —to live by the Golden Mean. I can't give to others more than I have. I begin every day alone doing what I believe is best for me, and then I'm ready to be useful to my love and others. If I want to be a light to others, I first have to be a light to myself. Once we grow to understand our true self, we can meet others from our center to theirs. When we honor our differences, one to another, we're capable of great happiness.

ACCEPTING THAT THE CORE OF YOUR
BEING IS AS PRECIOUS AND
WONDERFUL AS THAT OF ANY OTHER
PERSON IS THE GREATEST GIFT YOU
CAN EVER GIVE YOURSELF.

Joan Borysenko

Surround Yourselves with Mutual Friends

21

FRIENDSHIP NEEDS A
COMMON PARALLELISM OF LIFE,
A COMMUNITY OF THOUGHT.

Henry Adams

The secret for all lovers is that you put each other first. Everything else falls into place after this commitment. Love me, love my lover. Once you are partners, you have to rethink the ways you stay in touch with friends. There is nothing quite as wonderful as a couple having mutual friends with whom they like to spend time and make celebrations.

Some of us have friends who go back to our early days. As we evolve, we continuously meet new people with whom we share common interests and beliefs about life's deepest meaning and purpose. Some of the friends we've had over many years we may have outgrown. While we still want to "be friends," we have to decide how to share these friendships with our lover, if appropriate. Why hurt old friends' feelings unnecessarily? Rather than seeing them couple to couple, either see them alone or at a larger gathering.

Aristotle wrote realistically about friendship. He is insightful about what often happens with good, old friends, or buddies. "One has remained a boy in mind, while the other has become a man of high ability," he observes. "How can they continue friends?" This is a good question that couples must seriously consider. Once we become lovers, two souls intertwine.

Without hurting anyone's feelings, how can we be loving, fair, and reasonable as we join our lover's friends into *our* intimate circle? Our partner's friends were not our friends, our friends were not our lover's friends. No one wants to give up a friend. Have you felt some unease as you've tried to do the right thing to honor and love your partner without making sacrifices and compromises about friends?

Peter and I both have good friends and have been blessed by the new friends we've met since we've been together. We seem to be attracted to like-spirited people with whom we share a wide range of interests. Many of the friends we've made together are our best friends, no matter where they live all over the world.

When we are a couple, our friendships are nourished by mutual communication and respect for our partnership. I was invited to dinner years ago with a woman who announced, "I like Peter and all that but I'd rather spend the evening alone with you if that's all right." No, it was not all right. There is no way I'm going to ditch my husband on a Tuesday evening to go dine with someone else. I am too mature for play dates. I acknowledge that people have different points of view about seeing their friends without their partner tagging along, but I disagree. Life together is short and precious. Whenever possible we see our mutual friends together.

If a friend loves me, I hope that person can appreciate my significant other. When friendships are mutually embraced, there is no tension. It is joyful to be together in mutual pleasure to share different memories as we create new ones. When you have mutual friends, all four people are equally rewarded and appreciated.

How often each of you sees certain friends should never be determined by your partner but by mutual understanding and agreement.

Each person has friends who are important, but one partner should not sacrifice his or her time for the other's friends if they are not mutual. If there is not mutual compatibility, see your friends alone when your partner is away on a business trip or engaged in other activities. Make a date well in advance to see a friend in order for your partner to be able to arrange to see someone else at the same time. Think carefully if it is appropriate to give up precious time with your lover to be with a non-mutual friend.

With few exceptions I think as responsible committed lovers we can strike a balance where we enthusiastically share our time with mutual friends who make each of us equally happy. We should not merely tolerate our social experiences by overextending ourselves or dissipating our energies.

Some friends may be our friends for life because of our loyalty, but when we're with them they may be a drag on our energy because of their negative outlook on life. The thirteenth-century Persian poet Rumi warns us, "Do not sit long with a sad friend. When you go to a garden do you look at the weeds? Spend more time with the roses and jasmine." Try to make your visits compassionate and short. Thomas Jefferson wisely said, "The happiest moments my heart knows are those in which it is pouring forth its affections to a few esteemed characters."

We are blessed to have true friends with whom we can communicate and share all things. We need to strike a healthy balance between spending time with mutual friends and being alone enough as a couple for intimate private periods. Ideally we will grow to delight in sharing our friends as partners.

FRIENDSHIP OF A KIND THAT CANNOT EASILY
BE REVERSED TOMORROW MUST HAVE ITS ROOTS IN
COMMON INTERESTS AND SHARED BELIEFS.

Barbara Tuchman

22

Don't Discuss Your Intimacy and Secrets with Others

W henever you talk about your private matters with others, you are violating trust and confidence. You may be offending your lover when you break this honor code. You have one confidant with whom you can disclose your secrets and private matters. Be extremely guarded about this sacred trust.

Your personal affairs are no one else's business. Any slight indiscretion fuels gossip, spreading rumors that can be harmful. It is appalling when someone freely discusses personal details about their lover. I always feel quite uncomfortable when I am told negative things by one partner about the other. This behavior is almost always inappropriate and unacceptable. What goes on behind closed doors is between two people only.

We have to work things out together. When you talk to someone other than your partner (unless seeking professional help), you are off your path. No one else knows all the facts. Few people (if any) can keep a secret. Even if you don't tell secrets or reveal personal information, rumors have a way of getting started. I remember when Peter had emergency knee surgery due to a harsh fall on limestone at a show-house many years ago, and we had to cancel eight cities from our book tour. Some years later, we met a woman who whispered to me, "I'm so happy to see Peter looking so well. I've prayed for him ever since I heard he had a stroke." How ordinary knee surgery ends up in the brain is a mystery. I laughed and thanked Sally for her prayers. She told me, somewhat abashed, that she wished she'd known it was Peter's knee, and not something more serious.

Most often when someone discusses intimacy and secrets, it's disparaging of their partner. Anything negative about one of you reflects badly on you both. Wise are those who never sully their own nest.

We are thoughtful also when we don't tell all to our children or parents. They worry about us and tend to give unwanted advice. In most cases, it is better to stick together in private unity, working through challenges as well as celebrating moments of bliss. Loved ones are happiest when we're able, on our own, to work things out. Everyone has their own struggles, and we should all concentrate on how we can improve our own situations.

Being able to keep your secrets will assure mutual confidence and deepen your love. You are blessed; you have each other.

THREE MAY KEEP A SECRET,
IF TWO OF THEM ARE DEAD.
Benjamin Franklin

23

Be There as a Support for All Important Occasions

LOVE MAKES EVERYTHING THAT IS HEAVY LIGHT.

Thomas à Kempis

Once committed to lasting love, we will all go through sad, painful times together when loved ones and family members get sick and die. While we try to be supportive of each other in all circumstances, it is especially important to be a loving presence in the most difficult times. These troublesome experiences bring family members together who perhaps aren't close and haven't seen each other for a long time. When we feel the tension in these trying periods, there is a tendency to make excuses as to why we can't be there; it's sometimes easier to evade reality. It's a whole lot easier to be together at weddings and graduations than at hospitals and funerals, but we have to be there for all important occasions in order to demonstrate love in action.

Unhappy occasions can bring out the worst in some people. I remember misbehavior at a sad family event where I had to tell a self-absorbed, hostile teenage girl please not to say anything unless it was positive and constructive. She furiously huffed off from the restaurant dinner table and sat in the car for the rest of the evening. If there is uneasiness and strain beforehand, it tends to come out in times of uncertainty and sadness. But we are called on to give solace in times of trouble or sorrow, as well as to be there in the happy times.

If a loved one is suffering in mind or body, our tenderness and reassurance will make a huge difference to lessen the pain. Peter and I have the power to calm each other in these tense times of grief. Just his being at my side is a source of consolation, giving me hope and reminding me that we have each other's love, no matter what happens.

I disagree with Mark Twain who insisted "grief can take care of itself but to get the full value of a joy you must have someone to divide it with." When we remind each other how blessed we are to love and be loved, to have and to hold, to lift each other up, grief eventually transcends into acceptance because of this dependable bond shared through sickness and in health. When we are a light bearer to others, our compassion is a strong force for healing. Love spreads light, and the weight of a heavy heart can unburden when love is visible.

For that matter, it may not always be our idea of fun to attend the weddings or graduations of our spouse's family and extended family, nor the office holiday party or the college reunion. Sometimes you need to show your loving support if it's important to your partner that you be there (and you'll sense this even if your lover doesn't say so). Go and participate with goodwill. It will be much appreciated and it is appropriate to show support by your presence.

Be there as a support for all important occasions. Moral excellence is the ultimate definition of happiness. Keep this noble goal present in all the unpredictable, unfortunate times when we're needed to help our lover keep perspective and remain full of faith and hope. Love is the channel that makes all things work out as best as possible. Everything that happens should be a learning experience we can grow through together.

WHAT DO WE LIVE FOR IF IT IS
NOT TO MAKE LIFE LESS DIFFICULT FOR EACH OTHER?
George Eliot

24

A Home Has No Boss

WHERE LOVE RULES, THERE IS NO WILL TO POWER,
AND WHERE POWER PREDOMINATES,
THERE LOVE IS LACKING.
THE ONE IS THE SHADOW OF THE OTHER.

Carl Jung

Love rules at home. No matter who you are or how important your job, home is not run like a business or profession. When either person enters their home, each should do whatever possible to make their partner happy.

The early American novelist Louisa May Alcott wrote that "women have been called queens for a long time, but the kingdom given them isn't worth ruling." Home should not be a domestic trap where one partner runs the show and barks orders to the other. I know several women who are afraid of their significant other because the men are demanding perfectionists with impossibly high standards, enforced at the other's expense. Most of us don't appreciate being bossed around; we want to be loved and adored.

Queen Victoria and Prince Albert were deeply in love; a journal entry from February 11, 1840, is an intimate glimpse into this happiness: "Really, I do not think it possible for anyone in the world to be happier, or as happy as I am. He is an angel, and his kindness and affection for me is really touching . . . What I can do to make him happy will be my greatest delight." Through the exchange of kindness and love, the desire to serve is nurtured.

I don't believe in playing gender roles. The more freedom a woman has, the more freedom a man will have, because whenever anyone suppresses another, love is not present. Before Peter and I married, we had a serious discussion about how we would manage our home life. Peter reassured me that he didn't want to marry me to make me his housekeeper; he told me he wanted to live in love together, each helping out in the best ways possible. He assured me that together we would work out the necessary details of combining children from previous marriages.

Life runs more smoothly, more gently, and more happily when you forgo the boss role at home. I called a surgeon friend when I was preparing to give a speech to some doctors at a teaching hospital in Long Island. To my surprise, Anthony told me about the mistakes he'd made as a young doctor working hard to build his practice. He confessed he often brought the stress of the hospital home. His key advice was to remember who you are. "You are first a person, then a lover, a father, and a grandfather." Anthony's advice to these young physicians was to "go home and be present for your spouse and your children."

Love is always humble, generous-spirited, and thoughtful. When we're nurturing our home life, we're boosting happiness for ourselves as well as for our soul mate. There should be no hierarchy at home.

NO MAN IS GOOD ENOUGH
TO GOVERN ANOTHER MAN
WITHOUT THAT OTHER'S CONSENT.

Abraham Lincoln

25

It Feels Good to Look Good

THE SUDDEN DESIRE TO LOOK
BEAUTIFUL MADE HER
STRAIGHTEN HER BACK.
BEAUTIFUL? FOR WHOM?
WHY, FOR ME, OF COURSE.

Colette

I'd rather dress up than down. My father was a dress designer and manufacturer when I was a teenager. Although I was a tomboy, I grew up with an appreciation of the beauty and refinement of well-designed clothes made of quality materials. I enjoy the way my clothes allow me to express my personal energy, mood, and style. I feel more vibrantly alive when I wear clear, saturated colors—hot pink, apple green, cobalt blue, lemon yellow, and saffron.

It always feels good to look good. People usually know when they look well put together. Our sensory system becomes engaged. We get a physiological and psychological lift. This positive energy radiates to the world. When you dress well, you have a tendency to be more outgoing, resulting in meeting more interesting people. Many people somehow feel more comfortable when they dress down; however, how you dress does make an immediate impression on others, for better or worse. You don't have to be a clotheshorse to look good, but it is important to recognize how looking well can increase happiness for two.

Perhaps we should examine our dress code at home. When we are lovers, we spend an inordinate amount of time alone, together. We see no one else but each other. Out of self-respect and honor for your partner, it is wise to be thoughtful about how you look when you are alone.

From observation, I realize that many couples let down at home when they shed their public persona. Men take a rest from shaving; women rest their makeup-free skin. This relaxed period of time to unwind does not have to become grubby, where you wander around unfit and sloppy. How can a lover suggest that her love get out of his sweats? "You look like you've had a nice run." When translated, it means, "Yuck, go take a shower and put on some nice-looking clean clothes." How we present ourselves when we are alone, together, is an expression of esteem for our partner. One way to keep our love alive is to clean up our act when we're at home. Rather than always dressing down, there should be times when the spirit moves us to dress up. We should care enough about ourselves and our partner to feel good because we look good, even when we're not in the public eye.

I derive great pleasure from seeing Peter in an attractive bathrobe, nightshirt, or pajamas. It is enjoyable to see some colorful boxer shorts in plaids or stripes. I also enjoy the colors and patterns when I do the laundry. I have a collection of colorful nightshirts, pajamas, and bathrobes. Whenever possible I wear colored bras and panties, just to add zest. I have some sensuous "at home" long robes that are wonderfully comfortable and appropriate when we're alone at home for the evening. What we wear "at home" is as important as what we wear when we're not at home.

When we're conscious of how our own spirits and mood elevate when we make an effort to look good, we can take this simple step to enhance our sense of well-being whether at home or out on the town.

FOR GOODNESS' SAKE, FOR YOUR OWN
DIGNITY, *DRESS UP, NOT DOWN*!
TO ENLIVEN YOUR SPIRITS
AND LIFT THOSE AROUND YOU.

June Speight

When You Are Together, Be Together

THE EXPLOSION OF LOVE . . . KNOWS
NO SEPARATION.

J. Krishnamurti

When we're deeply in love, we never feel we spend enough time together, especially when business travel separates us. Our experiences together are precious. Peter and I have some of our happiest moments sitting by a warm fire, talking and sharing ideas. Heaven is not a place, but a raised consciousness. When we value these times of tender connection, we should aim to have every meeting be a mutual engagement.

Be there! When you are together, be present where you are. The Russian writer Leo Tolstoy advised, "If you want to be happy, *be.*" There are times when you both must bring the office home. We all have deadlines and periods when you'd rather be together than separated; but in order to avoid misunderstandings, make it clear in advance that you are bringing work home with a tight deadline looming. Whenever possible when you are at home, turn off your cell phone, your beeper, and anything that plugs in. A BlackBerry has its place, but not when you are lovers alone, together. The writer Rollo May teaches this. "For being together," he says, means "being together in the same world; and knowing means knowing in the context of the same world." When we're able to really be together, we have the feeling of belonging, of being an important part of each other. When we show interest in each other *without interruptions*, we'll live with greater harmony.

Think of the simple ways you can "be" together even if only for several minutes. One of you can bring your love tea in bed in the morning. Peter and I lay out our clothes together. He draws my bath and we dress at the same time. In the evening after returning home from work, make a drink and sit together to discuss the day.

Rather than thinking about the times we're not able to be together or feeling sad about our good-byes, focus on *being* together when you are together and your hearts will expand in love.

TECHNOLOGY . . . THE KNACK
OF SO ARRANGING THE WORLD
THAT WE DON'T HAVE TO EXPERIENCE IT.

Max Frisco

Take Care of Your Own Health

DO NOT SHORTEN THE MORNING
BY GETTING UP LATE; LOOK UPON
IT AS THE QUINTESSENCE OF LIFE,
AS TO A CERTAIN EXTENT SACRED.

Arthur Schopenhauer

No one knows more about your body than you do. When we are alert to symptoms that something is not normal, we can take certain measures to self-heal. Our bodies work around the clock, without a break, to assure everything performs properly. I have great faith in the virtues of preventative medicine: It is preferable to a promised cure. Ideally, we don't become sick. Once ill, far too often, you are immediately prescribed drugs. Our culture is now much too dependent on pills for everything imaginable. The side effects from a great many medicines are worse than the diagnosed illness!

When we commit ourselves to doing whatever we can to heal, we will better understand the ultimate connection between our mind and body. Our mind has potential divine intelligence but must be trained to think the thoughts that will lead to more radiant health. We should be alert to the mind's influence on healing as well as the beneficial effects of our deliberate actions. Doing the things that are good for us allows our body to perform with its innate powers of restoration and order. By having a regime to eat properly and get regular exercise, we are acting responsibly to maintain our health. Often, time itself is the best doctor.

We can be happy as a couple even when we are facing health challenges because when we're happy we're in a better position to heal, even if we're unable to be cured. Recent surveys have shown that happiness is not based on outside circumstances but on our reaction, attitude, and commitment to focus on all that is good in our lives. When couples love each other they take care of each other. But we have to listen to our own body and pay attention because only we know our symptoms. When your love is sick it deeply affects both of you.

Dr. Karl Menninger, founder of Menninger Clinic, strongly believes, "You cannot really love yourself and do yourself a favor without doing other people a favor, and vice versa." Taking care of our own health is key to self-love and happiness together as a loving couple. When our body feels vital and agile and we're full of energy, this is a sign we understand the intimate mind-body synergy. The ancient Greek physician Hippocrates proposed we understand our body when we are healthy, "we must turn to nature itself, to the observations of the body in health and disease to learn the truth."

Many of us are caregivers to others. When we come to realize that we should treat ourself just as well as we care for others, we will better understand how to let the natural forces in our body heal our dis-ease. Health and happiness are the great, sometimes unrecognized, human blessings we share as lovers. When we are unhealthy or unhappy, however, we can learn from our situation and use all our inner resources to heal ourselves in order to experience the great joy that we can feel as a loving couple.

Few of us can understand everything about our body. We never achieve complete knowledge. But we can be moderate in our habits, get more sleep and exercise, and focus on our overall common-sense wellness. When we're content and happy, our body responds in kind and our love will feel glad to be present with our good energy. The connection between feeling well and happiness for two is unquestionable.

When you want to achieve great happiness for two, take better care of your health. When you remember how important your sense of wellbeing is to you and your lover, you are on a path toward greater health, happiness, and true wisdom.

TO WISH TO BE WELL IS A PART
OF BECOMING WELL.

Seneca

28

Share Sensuous Meal Preparation

LEARN HOW TO COOK! THAT'S THE
WAY TO SAVE MONEY. YOU DON'T SAVE IT
BUYING HAMBURGER HELPERS AND PREPARED FOODS;
YOU SAVE IT BUYING FRESH FOODS IN SEASON OR IN LARGE
SUPPLY, WHEN THEY ARE CHEAPEST AND USUALLY BEST,
AND YOU PREPARE THEM FROM SCRATCH AT HOME.
WHY PAY FOR SOMEONE ELSE'S WORK, WHEN IF YOU
KNOW HOW TO DO IT, YOU CAN SAVE ALL THAT MONEY
FOR YOURSELF?

Julia Child

When you share preparing a delicious dinner, you're sharing love in action. There is a joy in discussing the menu ahead of time and deciding what you both would appreciate cooking and eating. Cooking together is an excellent way of gratifying the senses. When properly understood, the entire process can become a mindful meditation.

Because meal preparation isn't an intellectual experience, this can be a time when you both come together to enjoy each other's company as you divide up the various tasks, entering into intimate conversation in the privacy of your kitchen. Sharing is key. To make this time enjoyable, you both should equally participate. No matter what work you performed during the day, this time should be relaxing because you're together doing something for yourselves.

Do not rush this process. Sensuous experiences need time to evolve naturally. Decide who will set the table. Because I am a more accomplished cook, Peter helps me by chopping ingredients or making a salad dressing. He enjoys serving drinks and likes to light the candles.

Happiness for two is always close at hand when our hearts are in tune. Some people like to cook more than others, but when we share the various tasks, it doubles the pleasure because we're cutting the work time in half. We become wise when we find fresh ways to create beautiful shared moments doing necessary things that benefit us mutually. When we prepare a meal with a loving heart, it nourishes our soul as well as our body.

When you both establish a rhythm in the kitchen, it is similar to a dance. There is a flow, a give and take, a sense of connection, of mutuality. Because you are both focused in the moment, the stress of the day disappears, and your senses awaken to the delicious smells, the sounds, the touch and taste of something you created together as you see all the ingredients combine into a meal you savor.

How often are you able to prepare sensuous meals together? Do you find this a pleasant, bonding time you look forward to as you anticipate a happy experience? Don't you find that it makes a huge difference to your mood and spirit when you set an attractive table? With some flowers and candlelight, the kitchen table is both practical and appropriate. We shouldn't make a big deal out of something we're both going to enjoy. The point is to share in this ritual and to make it as memorable as possible.

Remember, we all like to be served. When we wait on each other, we're expressing tenderness and understanding.

A JOY THAT'S SHARED IS A JOY MADE DOUBLE.

John Ray

29

Encourage Adventures

I'M NOT AFRAID OF STORMS,
FOR I'M LEARNING
HOW TO SAIL MY SHIP.

Louisa May Alcott

Happiness for two should be a daring adventure. How long have you been together? How many more years do you think you'll be alive and in good health, in love and thriving? If you had to choose between security and adventure, what would you most wish for?

I want more adventures in our lives together. Whenever we seek greater security, we deny the possibilities of the mysterious unknown. There are places to go, people to see, and exciting things to do. We should want more and greater things to happen to us and, when we experience them together, we will both become more fulfilled.

Do you feel you have an adventurous attitude? Do you tend to seek and find fresh opportunities and thrive on variety? Are you stimulated by change and new environments, meeting strangers and moving around? Last year Peter and I went on an extended book tour that started in Chicago in mid-January and lasted until June in Milwaukee. We loved our experience. It was exhilarating to travel from city to city, seeing friends, meeting readers, and making new friends. Many people, looking at us from the sidelines, would comment, "You must be exhausted." Not so. We had a great time, living completely in the moment, going along with whatever was available to us, appreciating a closeup look into communities and then moving on.

My bag is packed, I'm ready to go, passport handy. I'm restless for more action, more wonderful experiences. I love the journey, not just the destination. I often say in my lectures that we're all headed in the same direction. It's the adventure that makes our life full, rich, deep, and meaningful.

What are some unusual or exciting experiences you've had in the past year? One woman at a luncheon in Lake Bluff, Illinois, announced in front of her daughter that every year she was going on an adventure with her husband. This year they were going to Costa Rica to experience the rainforests. Next year they're going to Africa on a safari. The year after, perhaps Japan and China.

Peter has a collection of brass carriage clocks and winds them all faithfully but does not have them synchronized. I asked him why they were set at different times and with an adorable smile he explained, "It's later than you think." We are acutely aware of the preciousness of our happiness for two and time seems to gallop as we live our hours with deliberate intensity.

Peter and I are looking forward to a new, exciting chapter in our lives, one that will provide refreshing experiences that will be both stimulating and enjoyable. We now have this great opportunity to live on our own terms, to do what we wish to do, because, in our maturity, our lives have changed. We are free now, really, for the first time since we were married. The main reason we're changing our lives in a new direction is because we no longer are raising and educating our children. There is no reason to remain in the same apartment where Peter has lived since 1959 and brought up eight children—six of his and my daughters, Alexandra and Brooke.

We moved out of the neighborhood with schools and downsized to meet our current needs. We want fewer domestic responsibilities and a simpler life. We don't just live in New York City, we live in the world.

Think about your happiness for two and encourage adventure. When friends' youngest daughter went off to college, they went off to Australia. Why not? Break free from your former patterns as your freedom unfolds and embrace the liberty by daring adventures. I'm ready to go. We both are. Are you?

LOVE DANCES IN THE
FRESHNESS OF THE UNKNOWN.

Deepak Chopra

30

Temper Your Temper

THE GROWTH OF WISDOM
CAN BE ACCURATELY
GAUGED BY THE DROP
IN ILL TEMPER.

Nietzsche

The good life is lived by the universal principles of doing what is good for you—and what is good for others. Happiness for two requires that we "temper our temper" for our own sake as well as for our loved one. To be around a person who has a fierce temper is offensive, disagreeable, and unpleasant.

Who among us has never lost their temper? We all know the dangers of this territory. But if someone has a fiery temperament, this person can be ferocious and even become violent. Humans are thinking animals who have free will, but we can be unthinking, rude, brutal, and uncultivated. Aristotle recognized that we can have legitimate reasons to become angry and experience strong feelings of displeasure, resentment, hostility, and injustice. But he urged us to be angry at the right person, at the right time, for the right reason, and in the right proportion.

Happiness and misery depend as much on temperament as on fortune, declared François La Rochefoucauld, the seventeenth-century philosopher and wit. A character trait I admire in a person is an even temper with a good disposition. When someone isn't irritable, we are in a better position to be open and relaxed. Self-restraint is essential for lasting happiness. To be happy and share happiness, we need to control ourselves in order to do what is best for others. Thomas Jefferson thought it through: "When angry, count to ten before you speak; if *very* angry, a hundred."

The master State Department diplomat George F. Kennan said that heroism is endurance for one moment more. If you feel you are about to explode, count to a hundred and also do deep breathing. Whenever I'm provoked, I breathe in my mantra, "love & live happy." I breathe out "love & live happy," and I go for a good long walk to clear my head.

Our ability to temper our temper lies in our skill at keeping our mind still. When we become serene inside, we calm down. I recommend any form of meditation where you can contemplate, reflect, and train yourself to empty your mind. One of my favorite ways to unwind is by doing "walking meditation." Meditation is a useful tool to use any time, wherever you are, to calm yourself.

What calms you? What are some of the things you instinctively do to soothe your nerves? Think of all the things that temper your temper:

- Go to the gym.
- Arrange flowers.
- Read ancient philosophy.
- Listen to favorite music.
- Prune the garden.
- Walk on the beach.
- Read a favorite storybook to a child.
- Watch an old movie.
- Make your favorite pasta dish.
- Swim.

- Polish silver.
- Clean out a messy drawer.
- Clear your desk.
- Fold clothes.
- Wash the car.
- Mop the kitchen floor.

When we can control our emotions, we're free to be more loving. Think of the big picture of all the good in your life and all the good you can do right now by being calm and happy.

THE SAVAGE IN MAN IS NEVER
QUITE ERADICATED.

Henry David Thoreau

31

Run Errands Together

NO MATTER WHAT YOU ARE DOING,
KEEP THE UNDERCURRENT OF HAPPINESS.
LEARN TO BE SECRETLY HAPPY WITHIN YOUR
HEART IN SPITE OF ALL CIRCUMSTANCES.

Paramahansa Yogananda

Everyone is in a hurry. Couples often feel they have to divide chores in order to conquer. Dividing chores may be good division of labor, but it also divides the family: He goes here and there, she goes here and there and then some, and they both go crazy. I'm a true believer in sharing domestic responsibilities because whenever you run errands together, they become grace notes because you're with each other. Peter and I tend to do most necessary things together because we enjoy ourselves, even when we go to the post office, a place where there aren't usually a lot of laughs.

Happiness for two is not about efficiency. Partners must keep reminding each other that their lives together should be far more nobly spent than in crossing things off their "to do" list. When you're in the swing of love, all the logistics are accomplished in a more lighthearted, easy manner.

Peter and I break up our errands with a "carrot." We weave treats into the process. We often do grocery shopping or stop at the pharmacy after supper out or on our way home from a movie or lecture because it is so convenient. Or we'll break up the errands with a stop for coffee at a nearby café where we can talk or read and get off our feet for a few minutes.

When lovers are together, they are in union no matter where they are or what they're doing. Sharing errands is a practical way of enjoying the process of your journey together. Whenever you are together, you share the same experience. You have a common understanding of how things worked out, who went out of their way to help you, who was unpleasant, and who you met along the way. In these small details, a common history is forged. Whatever the circumstances, whenever we are together we can feel grateful and calm, knowing all is well with us.

When possible, bring your young children with you on your errands. When I was raising my daughters in New York, I took them everywhere I could, including visits to my interior design clients. Once Alexandra and I were in a fancy chandelier shop while an uptight senior decorator at our firm was there with a client. I was later punished by the office manager for bringing my child with me, but I have no regrets because the more time we spent together, the better off we were.

Most of life is made up of little things. To miss doing these errands together is to miss everything.

TRIFLES MAKE THE SUM
OF LIFE.
Charles Dickens

32

White Lies Are Always Dangerous

HE WHO PERMITS HIMSELF TO TELL A LIE ONCE,
FINDS IT MUCH EASIER
TO DO IT A SECOND AND THIRD
TIME, TILL AT LENGTH IT BECOMES
HABITUAL; HE TELLS HIS LIES WITHOUT
ATTENDING TO IT, AND TRUTHS WITHOUT THE
WORLD'S BELIEVING HIM. THIS
FALSEHOOD OF THE TONGUE LEADS TO THAT
OF THE HEART, AND IN TIME DEPRAVES
ALL ITS GOOD DISPOSITION.

Thomas Jefferson

D o you think a white lie is "a trivial, harmless, or well-intended untruth" as stated in the American Heritage dictionary? An untruth is something false, it is a lie. When someone falsifies, there is dishonesty, distrust, and deception. White lies diminish our being a dependable, reliable, trusted, loving person.

Honesty seems to be the character trait people most admire in themselves or others. According to my informal survey on character and the results described earlier, honesty was the most important virtue. During my book tour for *You Are Your Choices*, I asked several hundred people how they felt about white lies. Some people said telling white lies was harmless if it meant they didn't have to hurt someone's feelings by being brutally honest. Perhaps you can envisage similar exceptions, but remember, lies are lies. There may be a time and place for them but they should be very, very rarely used in a close relationship. I believe that white lies among lovers ultimately are unloving. We deserve to know the truth. How else can we know how to act intelligently and virtuously? If you want to know, I too want to know.

I believe in telling the unvarnished truth as a loving partner. Be pure in your intention to state reality with no effort to disguise. There are no times when a white lie does one a favor. White lies tie you up in inconsistencies. Your memory fades; you offer a mix of misstatements. Whenever anyone dissembles, they are worse off than if they tell the truth. Honesty, without exception, is the best decision because you are always, no matter what the situation, true to your authentic self. Truth is powerful and always effective; white lies can kindle big lies that block out truths.

When your partner asks you a frank question such as "Do I look good?" that gives you the opportunity to evaluate the situation and, if appropriate, ask to see another scarf or necktie. If your love gives you a gift you find hideous, it is wise to be sincere and say, "It's not me." When you both are in the habit of always being true to your word, it attunes you more to each other. You feel connected on a more meaningful level.

When my best friend was dying of cancer, her doctors and husband lied to her about her perilous condition because they didn't think she could handle the truth. "Why didn't you tell me?" was her cry, but too late. Whenever you deeply love someone, there are ways to be genuine while being compassionate and kind.

OH, WHAT A TANGLED WEB
WE WEAVE, WHEN FIRST WE
PRACTICE TO DECEIVE!

Sir Walter Scott

33

Write Love Notes

WHAT COMES FROM THE HEART,
GOES TO THE HEART.

Samuel Taylor Coleridge

Several years ago I read a poignant article about a couple who had been married for forty-six years and were inseparable. One night while Marion was putting the finishing touches on the dinner preparations and William was playing the piano in the adjoining room, she died suddenly. The loss was devastating.

After months in shock, William realized he didn't have a single note or love letter from Marion—not even cards from when they exchanged gifts—because they were always together. Even though there were photographs and videos, he longed to see Marion's handwriting and feel her presence and her love expressed in tender words.

I felt William's grief and was deeply touched by his situation. I was reminded of the writer Dr. Samuel Johnson who mused, "An odd thought strikes me: we shall receive no letters in the grave."

Peter and I have been known to sit in the same room writing each other love notes for our anniversary or Valentine's Day or for a holiday, New Year's Day, or just because the spirit moves us. Peter has saved every love letter, note, and card I've ever sent or given him, and I have saved every one of his. A love note is a concentration of your deepening affection, providing a permanent reminder of mutual love.

When you save these treasured intimate love notes, you can browse through them from time to time. The writer Rollo May believes, "No one ever has enough love." Writing love notes regularly is a way of reinforcing your affectionate feelings. Write spontaneously from your heart. The English poet Percy Bysshe Shelley only lived to the age of thirty, but he left behind loving words: "Feel the love for those you adore, and express it with fervor."

Write love notes while your lover is alive and you are together. To inspire your poetic spirit, read more romantic poetry to set your heart aflame:

> Edna St. Vincent Millay
> Elizabeth Barrett Browning
> Robert Browning
> Emily Dickinson
> John Keats
> William Wordsworth
> Henry Wadsworth Longfellow
> Robert Frost
> William Butler Yeats

Jean-Jacques Rousseau, the eighteenth-century French philosopher, instructs us "to write a good love letter you ought to begin without knowing what you mean to say, and to finish without knowing what you have written." Write with enthusiasm and divine inspiration. Just do it. Put pen to paper and let the muse channel through you as your heart yearns to connect more deeply in love's mysteries. Keep your words simple. The truth is the prize that will shine brightly.

"I love you" is always appropriate and appreciated. Do you love me, too? Write me a love note. What greater gift can I receive?

AT THE TOUCH OF LOVE, EVERYONE
BECOMES A POET.

Plato

34

Give the Gift of Eye Contact

THEY SHALL SEE
EYE TO EYE.

Isaiah

My heart melts when Peter looks into my eyes. Eye contact is a gift because when we look at each other, we are engaging our souls. We look into someone's inner beauty and experience their goodness. The emerging field of social neuroscience is based on the idea that human brains are designed to interact. In these moments of connection, you are literally on the same wavelength, emotionally in perfect union.

In his book *Social Intelligence: The New Science of Human Relationships,* Daniel Goleman discusses how our brains are "wired to connect." If a loved one is supportive of you while you are doing something stressful, you feel better and it literally calms the brain circuits that produce stress hormones. We influence each other's moods more than we ever realized. Over a lifetime, our interactions have physical consequences, influencing others' health and overall well-being.

Goleman says that since "trivial interactions can affect a person's physiology, somehow you have to take them more seriously." When we come to understand the powerful gift of our eye contact, we can improve our nonverbal communication and feel intimately connected in silence.

When someone looks deeply into our eyes, we feel comforted without being interrupted. We feel a shared empathy. Eye contact is an excellent way to become attuned to your lover's emotions as you seek to understand how he's feeling.

Rejection hurts. When someone pretends not to have peripheral vision and doesn't look at you, this can cause social pain. When you're in a social situation, it is insulting to be speaking with a person who's looking around the room as if to find someone more interesting or important. Simple eye contact shows respect and acknowledges the presence of the other person.

When talking or listening, try to maintain eye contact regardless of the distractions around you. This total focus intensifies your time together.

When you lean toward each other with the gift of eye contact, a tender glance, or kind word, you may be surprised by a spontaneous kiss, or your love reaching over to hold hands. Eye contact is a gift you give yourself as you share a sensuous present moment.

WORDS ARE ONLY PAINTED FIRE;
A LOOK IS THE FIRE ITSELF.
Mark Twain

35

Mess Up, Clean Up

[CHAOS IS] A ROUGH, UNORDERED
MASS OF THINGS.

Ovid

Living is a messy business. Everything we do makes a mess, whether we are baking muffins with the children, cooking spaghetti, building a bookcase, working on a photo album, or writing a book. We will mess up our space whenever we're fully engaged in living well.

Happiness for two depends on both of you agreeing that when someone makes a mess, he cleans it up. It is not the mess that is frustrating to the other person, but the lack of cleaning up afterward. Some projects go on a long time, and the mess is there as an annoyance to your partner.

As soon as the project is over, a thorough cleaning up and ordering of the space is a kindness. If some hobbies are ongoing—woodworking, sewing, quilting, or painting—there should be a designated space set up for these projects.

When I was raising my young daughters, doing puzzles was one of our play activities; I used cleanup as a teaching tool to show the girls that it's fun to put the puzzle away so it's ready for the next time the spirit moves us to do puzzles or word games or any other activity.

If our partner offers to cook dinner, it might be understood that we are going to do the dishes together, or perhaps you both share in the meal preparation as well as in the cleaning up. But one person should not be burdened by someone else's mess.

After we complete a project, we should take pleasure in putting things back in order. If you are engaged in something you can't complete in a short amount of time, try to contain your private mess to your own work or study area in order not to turn the general spaces into a disorderly accumulation of papers.

The kitchen table, the counters, and the dining room table should be cleaned up in order for the flow of meal preparation and eating not to be disturbed by having to clean up before messing up and then cleaning up again. Mess blocks our energy. Encourage each other, children, and grandchildren to freely mess up as they enthusiastically work and play, and allow time for putting everything away in good order. No home can ever be habitually clean and neat. A spotless, always immaculate house is a dull environment for our creative spirit to rise. When we don't demand perfect neatness, we find our mutual happiness to come naturally. Live well and mindfully together in concrete as well as spiritual ways.

Put down drop cloths, protect surfaces from damage. Get down and dirty, have fun, and take pleasure and pride in cleaning up your own mess.

EXAMPLE IS NOT THE MAIN
THING IN INFLUENCING OTHERS.
IT IS THE ONLY THING.
Albert Schweitzer

36

Offer to Help

IN ABOUT THE SAME DEGREE
AS YOU ARE HELPFUL YOU WILL
BE HAPPY.

Theodore Reik

The most gracious thing a person can do is sincerely offer to help in various situations rather than stand around and assume that no help is needed. When you offer to help your partner, it shows awareness and sensitivity. When Peter offers to help me, I'm grateful and it relieves me of feeling I'm carrying too heavy a load. I become less needy and feel supported when I'm asked, rather than when I have to say, "Would you please [do something specific]." There seems to be a release on both sides when we genuinely offer to help.

Very often we're in the rhythm of what has to be done and we don't need help when offered, but we love to know that the thought is there, showing care. We feel better when someone recognizes our efforts. Any form of benevolence toward each other where we give assistance and relief is useful and kind.

We feel better ourselves when we do something for others. Dr. Karl Menninger's advice to a man who said he was going to suffer a nervous breakdown was: "Lock your house, go across the railroad tracks, and find someone in need and do something for him." All our accumulated charitable acts are stepping stones toward greater happiness for two.

We lift ourselves up on angels' wings when we lighten the burden of others.

Albert Schweitzer, the twentieth-century French philosopher, taught us that "the only ones among you who will be really happy are those who will have sought and found how to serve." Whenever we are helpful, we increase our own health and happiness; serving others is a joy shared.

Our help is needed. Offer to help with a willing heart. This mutuality of caring for and serving each other is the universal law of compensation where we carry the weight together. There is a give and take, a cause and effect to every action. The more we give, the more we receive. We help ourselves by helping out our partner. Giving help is the way we demonstrate active virtue.

The cornerstone of happiness for two is the joyful gift of our loving support, our presence, our assistance, and our attention to whatever the needs are: "What may I do to help you right now?"

> THIS IS OUR SPECIAL DUTY, THAT IF ANYONE
> ESPECIALLY NEEDS OUR HELP, WE SHOULD
> GIVE HIM SUCH HELP TO THE
> UTMOST OF OUR POWER.
>
> **Cicero**

37

Establish Your Own Rituals and Traditions

TRADITION IS LIVING AND ACTIVE,
BUT CONVENTION
IS PASSIVE AND DEAD.

Thomas Merton

Whenever we ritualize our lives as partners, we are honoring our union. The rituals and ceremonies each of us was raised to participate in are not necessarily appropriate for our lives as partners. We may have cultural or family traditions that are passed down from generation to generation that may not benefit our lives today. In reality, many rituals are rigid, making traditional ceremonies and celebrations command performances. Once you become a couple you have to gently but firmly put parents and one's old ceremonies aside or at least into a different place. Often, in truth, we want to honor others, but also be alone together. As independent adults we should create our own rituals as lovers.

Perhaps years ago, Sunday luncheon with your parents was an enjoyable and time-honored tradition. However, is anyone benefited if this ritual has become an obligation? Where do you go? Which set of parents is invited? Who do you try to please? Why are you still subjected to the same traditions you followed when growing up, now that you're grown up and living independently? You have to accept the reality that you've graduated.

While you establish your own rituals and traditions, you can also update traditions with others. Rather than rushing home from your weekend away to have Sunday brunch, perhaps you can tactfully suggest supper during the week. To take the burden off a sibling who always "does" the holiday meals, suggest everyone pitch in to reserve a private dining room at a restaurant.

Free yourself from feeling you are a victim of other people's expectations and demands. Most of us crave a moment's peace. The only way to claim our own freedom is to establish private rituals and ceremonies that you look forward to and know will not be violated.

When on vacation, make a point to watch the sunset with a glass of wine, alone together, even if you are traveling with others. Or, establish a "date night" once a week and let nothing interfere with it. Celebrate each other as you wish and find new ways to honor others if the old ways aren't working anymore.

Whether you walk to work as a couple each day or bike to town together to have breakfast, follow through on your plan. There are times to be together with others and there are times to break tradition and establish your own patterns. The pressures from others, no matter how well-meaning, can put pressure on your relationship. Gently, lovingly, you both have to establish your own fresh, meaningful rituals. Once you do, try never to break them. Periodically, if we all try to be more independent, totally loving, and understanding of our ultimate interdependence, we'll find greater happiness for two that will encourage harmony and increase love.

[TRADITION] CANNOT BE INHERITED,
AND IF YOU WANT IT
YOU MUST OBTAIN IT BY GREAT LABOR.

Thomas Stearns Eliot

Stop Disappearing

SILENCE BREAKS THE HEART.

Phyllis McGinley

If you need a break, say so. Communicate your needs, but don't simply vanish from sight. Disappearance can take many forms. Beyond physical disappearance, you could get caught up in a book, a project, or a worry and not be aware of how long you've been gone. When a partner disappears it can be rude, inconsiderate, and even cruel. You are a couple seeking greater happiness together; there shouldn't be these incidents of disconnection that worry the other person. It is wise to check in from time to time if only to report.

If something is wrong, you have to get to the bottom of it together. You should talk things out, not storm out of the house. Some people are not aware of how powerfully such behavior affects their partner. If you are in the midst of an argument, debating different points of view, rather than the discussion deteriorating and becoming contentious, reconciliation should always be on your mind, where you reestablish a close relationship between yourself and your partner.

If you become easily frustrated when someone disagrees with you, work on yourself rather than reacting by disappearing. A loving partner worries where his other half has gone, and, even trying hard to remain positive, can think the worst. If you really have to blow off steam, announce you're going for a walk to clear *your* head. This will clear the air.

Peter and I have a small courtesy rule between us. We always let each other know where we'll be. If we leave a room we're both in, we say where we're going. If I leave the apartment to do errands and Peter is not home, I leave a note by the front door, letting him know when I expect to return. If something comes up to delay me, I call him. This is sound common sense that has sustained our amicable relationship.

THE WORST SIN TOWARDS OUR
FELLOW CREATURES IS NOT TO
HATE THEM, BUT TO BE INDIFFERENT
TO THEM: THAT'S THE ESSENCE
OF INHUMANITY.

George Bernard Shaw

39

Keep Business and Personal Affairs in Order

THE FIRST AND BEST VICTORY
IS TO CONQUER SELF.

Plato

One of the often neglected ways we can love one another is to manage well our own business and personal affairs. When we conscientiously organize all aspects of our lives, we gain in both efficiency and self-respect. With everything in good order, we maintain necessary personal serenity.

There are certain things no one else can do for us. There are particular documents, private papers, and files we must put together ourselves. Find a place for everything that is important. We must continue to be responsible about our business and personal matters.

Set up a system that is easy to locate and understand. Whether you have help or you work on your own, you should know where everything is, and, in case of emergency, your partner should also have easy access to these vital documents.

We tend to be in denial, living day to day as though life were to last forever. However, when important documents are missing and we haven't planned ahead, it can cause pain and unnecessary suffering to ourselves as well as our lover. Peter, for example, has a file entitled, "To my true love" that, apparently, contains a letter to me, and tells me the status of things, where to find files and documents, and what to do in the event of an emergency or if he dies before I do.

Be sure you have your will up to date, amended in changing circumstances. Do you have a living will? Does your doctor have a copy? Where are your original certified birth certificate and marriage license? Where is the original deed to your house? If you own a co-op apartment, where do you store the stock certificate? Are your insurance payments up-to-date? Have you records of what is insured?

If you wish to have a obituary, write a draft and have copies of a photograph you may wish to be used and place them among your personal documents. You may choose to have your originals in a safe-deposit box you rent from your bank.

Do you have a copy of all your credit cards, front and back, as well as of your passport and driver's license? Keeping a "home" looseleaf notebook can be useful. You can have an index in the beginning listing the telephone numbers of all the people and companies currently providing you with services. This is an excellent way of having a record of what you do to improve and maintain your house or apartment, year by year. Your sources are invaluable to keeping your business and personal affairs in order.

You can live with greater inner peace and self-esteem when you are meticulous about your records. Make your wishes crystal clear. This is your life and no one else can satisfactorily make these decisions for you. No one is automatically entitled to what is yours without your written consent. Happiness for two is sustained by your preemptive thoughtfulness about the love of your life.

GOOD ORDER IS THE FOUNDATION
OF ALL GOOD THINGS.

Edmund Burke

40

Allow Each Other Freedom for Contemplation

A GOOD MARRIAGE IS THAT IN WHICH
EACH APPOINTS THE OTHER GUARDIAN
OF HIS SOLITUDE.

Rainer Maria Rilke

When writing my first book, *Style for Living: How to Make Where You Live You,* I wrote in coffee shops and libraries because I had two rambunctious young daughters and writing at home was impossible unless it was before they woke up or after they were asleep at night. I even wrote in a hospital where I landed with walking pneumonia. I trained myself to work for two hours every morning before I got the girls out of bed.

Between my full-time job at an interior design firm and raising my girls I was extremely busy, and at first the task of carving out time to write seemed insurmountable. But I discovered a great sense of inner peace by my habit of silence and solitude every morning. This was my free time to contemplate, go to a peaceful, quiet place inside myself for introspection and soul searching. Twenty-six books later, one of the great joys of my life is still this time alone at my writing table where I come face-to-face with a pad of blank white paper. I begin with meditation and reading, musing and getting in touch with my spirit-energy.

All character development begins within our heart and soul. It is in moments of contemplation that all the different parts of my life are drawn together inwardly. My health, welfare, happiness, and productivity are greatly dependent on my giving myself hours of freedom from others' expectations, schedules, deadlines, and interruptions.

This deep thinking can't be done on a computer or while doing chores or running errands. Each of us must protect ourselves and our partner in order to give this inner spaciousness a chance to flower. We need to escape our own busy-ness and the busy-ness of everyone else: remove ourselves from other people's stress and complaints and agitation, allowing ourselves peaceful calm moments of reflection.

When we ponder our lives thoughtfully, we will always find our center, even if we get off our path from time to time. Anne Morrow Lindbergh's classic 1955 book *Gift from the Sea* has guided me through many rough patches as I've tried to balance my life without shutting out my soul by being too busy or outer-directed. In Chapter Two, Anne wrote, "I understand why the saints were rarely married women. I am convinced it had nothing inherently to do, as I once supposed, with chastity or children. It has to do primarily with distractions . . . Women's normal occupations in general run counter to creative life, or contemplative life or saintly life." Aristotle believed that the highest form of happiness is the contemplative life, thinking about truth and beauty, not the life of excessive action.

Help guard your lover's privacy and need to be alone. Peter and I are able to share silences, making solitude for two possible. When I have a pen in my hand with the nib pointed at paper, Peter knows not to interrupt. It's not when I'm literally writing that noninterruption matters most, but when I'm thinking. When Peter is in a contemplative mood, I sense it and we don't talk. We need time and space to become one with our essence. The American Trappist monk Thomas Merton went further: "There is no true intimacy between souls who do not know how to respect one another's solitude."

Silence is golden. Shakespeare wrote in *Much Ado About Nothing* that "Silence is the perfectest herald of joy." In this contemplative state when you are alert and receptive you lose all sense of time and space, and you no longer wish to be in control. When two people love each other, they help each other in this exciting growth process. As we grow in under-standing our mind and soul are on fire, while, at the same time, we have inner peace and a sublime joy enters our essential nature. This must be nourished in lofty silence.

SILENCE IS A TRUE FRIEND WHO
NEVER BETRAYS.

Confucius

When Necessary, Be the Nurse

HEALING BEGINS WITH CARING.

Bill Moyers

The English pioneer-nurse Florence Nightingale taught that tending the physical needs of the sick is not enough. "The purpose of nursing," she wrote, "is to put the patient in the best condition for nature to act."

When either of us is under the weather, we find great comfort in our love being there in the same room. I remember one night when Peter was in the hospital after knee surgery. I got into his bed with him and we watched a movie on television. Of all our virtues, being a truly caring person is success in life. My nurse friend Carole believes that caring is our deep focus. When we empathetically concentrate, paying close attention to our loved one, we find a variety of ways we can, as Emerson suggested, make ourselves necessary to someone. The Buddha understood: "If you do not care for each other, who will care for you?"

Caring is a most important activity because it is love in action. When we're caring we're observant and mindful, considerate of our partner's needs. We're inclined to be happiest when we care and love deeply and are in a position to help. I feel it is a privilege and blessing to be there in sickness as well as in health.

The ancient Roman poet Virgil told us how to be useful. "Being myself, no stranger to suffering, I have learned to relieve the suffering of others." The fact is that there are times when each person in a committed relationship will need to be the nurse.

We ask questions in order to give the sick partner choices. Whenever I am ill Peter makes a list and goes out to do some errands, bringing back flowers and food that will lift my spirits and tempt my appetite. He brings me a variety of things to read, and often, he reads to me. Peter combs my hair, and rubs Molinard's Crème 24 on my arms and feet. He is cheerful as he gently caresses me. The touch of our lover when we don't feel well is both reassuring and healing.

We protect each other's privacy. Neither one of us ever wishes to have visitors when we are not feeling well. There is a sweetness in this calm, quiet atmosphere. We turn off the phone. We read and rest. Our fast-paced life slows down as we allow the debilitated body time to naturally heal. Happiness for two increases when we're able to drop everything in order to care for each other. Unless an illness is more serious, your favorite nurse is your true love.

THE CENTRAL PURPOSE OF EACH LIFE
SHOULD BE TO DILUTE THE MISERY
IN THE WORLD.

Karl Menninger

42

Bring Flowers Home

GIVE ME HANDFULS OF LILIES
TO SCATTER.

Virgil

I have a friend who shares my passion for flowers. Charles Masson, the proprietor of our favorite restaurant in New York City, La Grenouille, is also an artist, a writer, a gardener, and an avid appreciator of sheer beauty. Peter and I courted at this great classic French restaurant, founded by Charles's parents. We have celebrated all our important dates there not just because of the superb food, but because Charles's flower bouquets are over the top. He literally creates a garden in full bloom for his guests to experience. "Flowers," Charles once told me, "are for those fortunate enough to live fully every moment of their lives."

Last Valentine's Day, in Seattle, Washington, I gave a talk at the Northwest Flower and Garden Show entitled, "Stress Reduction Through Flowers." I spoke of the wondrous beauty of flowers, the joy of growing them, tending them, arranging them, and living with them in the rooms that we occupy. Emerson once said, "Earth laughs in flowers." I talked about Claude Monet's passion for flowers as I showed slides of his gardens at Giverny. At the book signing that followed, the flower and garden show owners gave a long-stemmed red or white rose to everyone who bought a copy. One woman told me she enjoyed my talk but was too frugal to buy flowers for herself. "Alexandra, how do you feel knowing that flowers are going to die?" I reminded her, "We are going to die, too. But while we're alive, flowers help remind us how mysteriously beautiful nature is and help us remain in awe of creation."

Heather bought a copy of my book, pointing out that because of the tulips on the cover, she was bringing flowers home. She selected a white rose. Heather told me her boyfriend was taking her out for dessert and espresso at a favorite café to celebrate Valentine's Day. "I'm going to bring my rose to enjoy our evening more before I bring it home to put by my bed. This one rose will inspire me to buy flowers for myself from now on."

An instant indoor garden can be created when we have fresh flowers in the house. Peter also loves living with fresh flowers. I adore it when Peter walks through the door with a bunch of tulips or daffodils he picked up from a grocery store on his way back from a meeting. Often when I buy flowers to bring home I have them wrapped in clear cellophane tied in a ribbon. I write a little note to Peter that makes the flowers a gift we'll both enjoy.

When we love flowers we can't afford not to bring them home. Flowers in our home greatly increase our happiness for two. You can buy one bunch and divide it into smaller vases to put in several rooms . . . or you can buy a single flower to put in a tall glass to enjoy in a place where you're likely to see it often. Whether you place a flower on your bedside table, the bathroom sink area, or the kitchen table, you will find great pleasure in this earthly delight. I move my small bouquets around from room to room. Whenever possible, put flowers in front of a mirror to double the bloom. If you leave home for a few days, place the vases in the refrigerator to help the blooms live until you return.

Several recent studies prove the positive benefits of fresh flowers in the home. Researchers went to nursing homes and delivered bouquets of flowers to certain residents. Not only were the elderly recipients more outgoing as a result of receiving the mysterious anonymously gifted bouquet, but their memory improved. They hugged and kissed the person who delivered the flowers, tended to invite people into their room to see the bouquet, and socialized more because their mood was elevated.

The only sad note about the researchers' completing their study is that the recipients of this largesse missed receiving flowers after the study ended, and their behavior returned to what it had been before the surprise flower boost.

Everyone knows how passionate I am about flowers. I'm fortunate to have realized that fresh flowers regularly at my home are a priority for our happiness for two.

THE AMEN! OF NATURE IS
ALWAYS A FLOWER.
Oliver Wendell Holmes, Sr.

Talk Up, Not Down

RIGHT BELIEF
RIGHT INTENTIONS
RIGHT SPEECH
RIGHT ACTIONS
RIGHT LIVELIHOOD
RIGHT ENDEAVORING
RIGHT MINDFULNESS
RIGHT CONCENTRATION

The Buddha, The Eightfold Path

There are two types of "talking up." First, you express the opposite of anything condescending. You try hard never to express to others a feeling that they are in any way inferior. Second, when you aim to "talk up," you speak kindly and positively.

The nineteenth-century English writer George Eliot wrote that "a patronizing disposition always has its meaner side." How true. Whenever someone talks down to us, they make us feel stupid. It shows lack of respect when someone treats another person in a condescending manner. Talking down shows the speaker's insecurity and low self-esteem. Another form of "talking down" is being blaming, making accusations, being negative, and finding fault, especially unfairly.

Whenever we talk in ways that are appropriate to our dignity, we will talk up and not debase our soul by talking down. In an intimate love relationship, the habit of expressing tenderness and support builds your lives together. "Kind words cost nothing and can be short and easy to speak," declared Mother Teresa, "but their echoes are truly endless." Unkind words are extremely costly because they destroy lives as they break hearts. When someone talks down to you, blaming and accusing you of something you've done or not done, the encounter too often degenerates into arguing and overbearing harangues; the truth is lost. The worst kind of talking down is when someone blames you for their own unhappiness! Everything suddenly becomes your fault. We're here to learn how to enjoy happiness for two and continuously affirm our life and the lives of others. Raw blame and finding fault are unloving.

I open up as though I'm a flower blossoming when Peter talks up, not down to me. We can train our mind to speak affirmatively, confirming all that is positive, all that will strengthen our commitment to be loving. By being more mindful of the words we select we can reject the negative, or anything that could be misinterpreted. Yale English professor William Lyon Phelps wrote poetically in his autobiography that we should "paint the walls of our minds with many beautiful pictures." Phelps talked up.

Make a list of all the "talk up" words, attitudes, or phrases that would make you or your partner feel appreciated, loved, and understood. Some might be:

generosity of spirit
thoughtfulness
assisting others
compliments
encouragement
supportiveness
a loving heart

compassion

empathy

grace

thankfulness

benevolence

service

helpfulness

understanding

optimism

hopefulness

providing tranquility

giving time for contemplation

patience

acceptance

Phrases

"I'm happy for you."

"Do whatever is best for you."

"I believe in you."

"I trust you."

"I love you."

"I cherish our time together."

"I support your decisions."

"Trust your intuition."

"You will always know what to do."

"I adore everything about you."

"I'm proud of you."

"You are doing a superb job."

"You are courageous."

"You are an angel."

"Thank you for organizing everything so well."

"You are the love of my life."

"You're really doing a good job, darling."

A doctor friend established the habit of talking up by reading more poetry. Robert assured me he developed the ability to "talk up" in three months and recommends this practice to his friends and peers. Train your mind to say words that will generate good energy between you and your love. Think of "E" words to talk up:

ENCOURAGE

EDUCATE

ENLIVEN

ENLIGHTEN

ENTERTAIN

ENERGIZE

EMPATHIZE

ENLARGE

ENRICH

ENTHUSE

Talk up. It is the "right" way to live. If you can't say something kind, bite your lip. Choose to point to and express the light.

LOVING WORDS TRULY
EXTEND THE JOY
OF TWO LIVES.

Peter Megargee Brown

44

Stop the Teasing

OF ALL THE GRIEFS THAT HARASS THE DISTRESSED
SURE THE MOST BITTER IS A SCORNFUL JEST.

Samuel Johnson

Teasing is really not funny. The teaser is making fun of you, not making fun, and enjoys undermining you. While a remark or two might initially appear innocent, it ends up as a toxic poke. Teasing keeps relationships insincere and superficial: Who can trust a tease with their deepest secrets?

I don't think teasing is ever acceptable because it sets someone up to look foolish. It is a mean way of finding fault, irritating an innocent person, or hurting their feelings. Teasing downgrades the teaser, as people who tease do it to knock you down in order to feel superior. When it goes too far, they smirk and say, "Just kidding; can't you take a joke?" People who like to tease tend to be insecure and cynical. Teasing can lead to quarreling, fault-finding, and a disruptive argument.

Be lighthearted, be a source of amusement and pleasure, be funny, but try never to use sarcasm or scorn, disguised as "just teasing." What you say in jest could be interpreted to be unloving. Teasing subverts trust and pulls us off the path of what is decent and good.

NEVER INJURE A FRIEND, EVEN IN JEST.

Cicero

45

Sincerely Say You're Sorry

THERE IS SOMETHING IN
HUMILITY WHICH
STRANGELY EXALTS
THE HEART.

Saint Augustine

The flip side of forgiveness is humility. Some people believe when two people love each other, you don't have to say you're sorry. I disagree. It is bad for *our* soul to not be kind and thoughtful. Whenever we are forgetful, impatient, or insensitive, saying something sharply critical, when we sincerely say, "I'm sorry," we clear the air. We empty our mind of negative thoughts.

Saying you're sorry when you mean it is soothing because it releases the other person from being upset. When we express our regret about something we wish could have been different, we're expressing our compassion and empathy. People who have difficulty saying they're sorry suffer from feelings of inferiority.

Until you genuinely say you're sorry, you're withdrawing your love while inflicting pain. When you're not sorry, you are not understanding the consequences of your behavior. There will always be reactions to everything we do or don't do. We pay a price whenever we've hurt someone's feelings by not being generous-spirited and sensitive to their wishes and needs.

It is better to say you're sorry even for a vague misunderstanding where you don't quite know how it happened. If you and your partner agreed to meet at a building entrance and you end up at the second of two entrances while your partner is waiting at the first, you may think you're right and your partner is wrong because you were at the main entrance on the avenue while your partner was at the street entrance, and you might feel ticked off because you were waiting more than twenty minutes in the cold.

But your lover was concerned about you, looking all around and waiting in the cold, too, and when you finally unite you should be glad you are both safe and together again. Be humble. Be sorry you were not where your partner thought you would be. Don't try to prove you are right and your lover was wrong. There are bound to be times of confusion and crossed wires. Someone hears or assumes one thing, the other something else. Right or wrong, we should show our love, not our sense of indignation. Remember what's important. No one who loves us deliberately plays games.

We all make mistakes. When we sincerely apologize, we should be forgiven. Focus on all the times you are in complete harmony. Whenever there is any slight disconnection, be eager to say you're sorry, be forgiving of yourself and your partner, and be grateful as you move forward.

THE HIGHER WE ARE PLACED,
THE MORE WE SHOULD BE HUMBLE.

Cicero

Encourage Each Other to Have More Fun

IF A MAN INSISTED ALWAYS ON BEING SERIOUS,
AND NEVER ALLOWED HIMSELF A BIT OF FUN AND
RELAXATION, HE WOULD GO MAD OR BECOME UNSTABLE
WITHOUT KNOWING IT.

Herodotus

M ost of us work hard. We live in an age of information overload and technology that allows us to be connected to our work and colleagues twenty-four hours a day. Life is serious and we have to keep up, compete, and excel. But we pay a price for this reality. Our work is never done. We multitask at great danger to ourselves and others.

We have to be aware of our need for balance and not go overboard in either extreme of all work and no play or vice versa. We should remind each other to be more playful. When we're lighthearted we're happy and carefree. Who wants to be around a drudge? Regularly encourage each other to have more fun, to do more things that are a source of enjoyment and amusement.

Pleasure, Aristotle suggested, is natural, desirable, and healthy. At a friend's wedding, the priest advised the couple to be good friends, to have a sense of humor and realistic expectations. When we're full of fun and spontaneous, we stay in touch with our playful nature. A husband who is crazy about his bride asked her after lunch at a favorite bistro in

New York City, "Hey, blondie, where are we going?" Spontaneous happenings are often the most loving and joyful. The twentieth-century American architect and inventor Buckminster Fuller challenged us to "dare to be naive." Being frolicsome and even silly from time to time is important.

When is the last time you were giddy-happy? How often are you playful? How humorous are you?

Often partners get into the habit of doing chores around their house on weekends. They make lists and plan ahead what duties they'll accomplish. If you only think of all the "shoulds," it could sound as though you don't want to have fun. How can you avoid getting bogged down? You can offer a solution: "Let's see how we can get these things done in order to join in the fun." Eliminate the word "chores" from your vocabulary because when you want to have fun, domestic tasks do not need to be unpleasant. Pleasure can always be found in the process, whatever you may be doing.

Every day we're together we should remind ourselves to remain in the consciousness of mutual joy. No matter how you were brought up, you can learn by practice to become more playful and have more fun together. Peter and I love to go on little jaunts we call grooves where we enjoy ourselves, feel delight and wonder. When the spirit moves us we go out to breakfast or we go to an art gallery exhibit. We enjoy going for a walk around the reservoir and the Boathouse in Central Park. In a snowstorm we love to put on boots and crunch along the avenue.

The novelist Ciji Ware wrote about lightening the emotional weight of possessions in *Rightsizing Your Life*. She and her husband left a large house and after many moves and storage bills they discovered where and how they wanted to live. They found a small beach cottage in California. "We're both working full speed," she wrote, "doing more than we ever did. It's great when you can move more lightly on the planet. You have much more time for fun." What a great metaphor for happiness for two: Encourage each other to move more lightly and have more fun.

TO MISS THE JOY IS TO MISS ALL.

William James

Don't Move Things from Each Other's Personal Spaces

THE PERSONAL LIFE OF EVERY
INDIVIDUAL IS BASED ON SECRECY,
AND PERHAPS IT IS PARTLY FOR
THAT REASON THAT CIVILIZED MAN
IS SO NERVOUSLY ANXIOUS THAT
PERSONAL PRIVACY SHOULD BE RESPECTED.

Anton Chekhov

For years Peter enjoyed spreading out his papers on his desk in the apartment living room. We both like to work in this room because of the space, light, art, and favorite objects. There was only one serious drawback. Every time we'd have friends over, I'd move all the clutter from his desktop to his office space off the kitchen. He felt disoriented when he didn't know where things were. "Things float," he'd say.

Eventually we were able to set up a practical work space with plenty of file cabinets and shelf space in a back office we call the "green room" because we painted it a rich hunter green. We've shared this office for years and each of us cleans off our living room desk surfaces before company arrives. The green room is then off-limits to wandering guests.

As a general rule, it is best never to move something from your partner's personal spaces without permission. You may be tempted, especially when you're in a clear-the-clutter mood, but don't. It's too controlling and invasive. Far better to mutually agree that personal space is private: Do not disturb! When I'm extremely busy, I make stacks of items that need my attention. It doesn't look organized but it is a work in progress and I can see what needs to be done. If you share a space, you can both neaten your own area at the same time, perhaps inspiring each other in the effort. Plato believed that once we acquired knowledge we would act wisely. Aristotle disagreed with his teacher, declaring that we don't always follow what we've come to know is best for us. Both philosophies seem to apply to cleaning up our spaces!

My system is to keep things in sight until they're dealt with. Peter tends to do the same. Until we've thanked someone for a gift or a letter, we don't put the item away because then we may forget to show our appreciation. Ideally, we shouldn't make too great a mess in our personal spaces because it saps our energy, but there are times when we have to accept reality and live for a while with an excessive amount of clutter, against our better wishes.

If one of you has a tendency to be neater than the other, be grateful your own private spaces are not violated. If you're fortunate to have someone come regularly to clean the house, be sure you've tidied up your personal items ahead of time. I put a scarf over the top of a desk in a hotel room in order not to have my papers disturbed when I'm not in the room.

Show respect for each other's privacy by never moving things from your partner's personal spaces. We should take charge of our own affairs and be assured privacy.

A PRIVACY OF GLORIOUS LIGHT

IS THINE.

Wordsworth

Encourage Self-Expression

A MUSICIAN MUST MAKE MUSIC,
AN ARTIST MUST PAINT, A
POET MUST WRITE, IF HE BE
AT PEACE WITH HIMSELF. WHAT
A MAN CAN BE, HE MUST BE.

Abraham Maslow

Show me what you like to do and I'll tell you who you are. When we give support to our partner's self-expression, we nurture the other's creative spirit that is the natural outlet of their unique personality. When people can't express themselves or go through a period when their flow of vital energy is blocked, they feel bottled up inside and, because they are thwarted, their frustration can lead to discouragement.

Peter and I enjoyed going to an inn in Connecticut for several years after we were married, and we met the American writer, artist, and profound thinker Eric Sloan at a wonderful restaurant nearby. Eric and his wife, Mimi, asked us to visit their lakeside house and studio. My young daughters, Alexandra and Brooke, went with us and were enchanted to visit Eric's studio to see his paintings and examine where he wrote his books longhand. We became friends and saw the Sloans on several occasions, even in Santa Fe, New Mexico, where we went on a buying trip for one of my decorating clients and they were there to attend an art opening of his paintings.

Over lunch one day Eric got up from the table after we were all fin-ished and announced, "I haven't done anything today. I must get to work." Eric, like many creative geniuses, had to express himself in order to be happy. At a writer's conference an aspiring writer asked a famous author if it was painful to write. The answer was clear: "It's painful not to write."

How often have you felt a great sense of relief and release when you're in the flow of writing a letter, or making an entry in your jour-nal, involved in an absorbing business project, or working on an article or essay or chapter of a book? When you're solving an interior design problem, sketching architectural details, engaged in a woodworking project, painting a still-life, or making a quilt, you feel focused and calm. Ideally we want to feel relaxed, free to express ourself and feel at peace. Studies show that when people are in what is called the flow state—focused and concentrating intensely on what they are doing, detached from their physical surroundings—they are happier than when they are aware of all the details and distractions around them. When we cross into this trancelike state, we can experience great clarity of self-expression.

It doesn't matter what we're doing as long as we're passionate about it. We all have certain gifts and talents that we love. These are natural ways for us to serve others. We are pure potential. To give our lives greater meaning, we should explore our interests and pursue them joy-fully.

What are some of your forms of self-expression?

    fabric design
    studying architecture
    weaving
    environmental conservation

horticulture and gardening

writing a memoir

painting

woodworking

writing poetry

taking piano lessons

studying modern dance

illustrating children's books

glassblowing

jewelry design

calligraphy

fashion design

faux finishing

becoming a chef

furniture design

bookbinding

making sculptures

editor

broadcaster

journalist

pundit

coach

teacher

philosopher

consultant

restaurateur

floral arranger

doctor

counselor

nurse

healer
minister
antiques dealer

There are some misguided people who feel self-expression is selfish. I believe we serve others best when we put our innate gifts to good use. If you are an artist, only you can paint your painting. If you don't express yourself, the world will never experience your unique vision. If you feel selfish being an artist because of the poverty and tragedy in the world, pick a cause, paint the painting and, depending on your economic condition, give all or a portion of the proceeds to clean water in Africa or to save horses from being slaughtered or to provide books to underprivileged children.

All self-expression requires self-discipline. Some of the best public speakers were petrified the first time they went up on a stage to the podium, only to discover that with training, discipline, and determination they could improve their skills, banish panic, and take pleasure in expressing their point of view in public. With the habits we develop, we put ourselves in the position to enter our flow state more often and can feel more confident that the muse will be there if we show up.

When we acquire the habit of self-expression, everything tends to fall into place. As we access our inner resources, we become less needy and more self-contained and self-sufficient. What are you meant to do that no one else can do? What's keeping you from encouraging each other's self-expression?

We must continuously encourage self-expression in each other. Your partner can get the children up so you can write in the morning. Let your lover disappear to the woodshop for supplies. Try to notice things your partner says that point to interests and exploration. Buy a book or magazine subscription or a pertinent gift certificate. Lend your support to any form of self-expression that uplifts your soul mate and others. Some people want to talk and write while others want to make things. Creators create, makers make. Whether we express ourselves making ceramic objects or through dance or music, know that you will both increase your happiness when each of you has found many creative, useful means of self-expression.

Abraham Lincoln knew the deepest truth: "Man was made for immortality." When we express the best that's inside us, we become incandescent; we glow and shine brightly. In his useful book, *Feng Shui Made Easy*, William Spear wrote, "Creativity lives in all of us, large and small, young and old. With it, life is magical." We harmonize with the flow of chi, our spirit-energy, when we encourage mutual self-expression.

EVERYONE HAS BEEN MADE FOR
SOME PARTICULAR WORK AND THE
DESIRE FOR THAT WORK HAS BEEN
PUT IN HIS OR HER HEART.

Rumi

49

When Treats Become Traps

EVERY INCREASED POSSESSION
LOADS US WITH A NEW
WEARINESS.

John Ruskin

Shakespeare asked a most intelligent question: "Can one desire too much of a good thing?" What's your answer to this question? What do you consider treats in your life? What is special, not something you do every day? What do you wish you could do more often? Are some of the things you now do, whenever the spirit moves you, former treats? Are good things always good? Are they good for you and others? If you're enthusiastic about life, is it possible to desire too much?

Yes. Too much of anything is too much. Even too much of a good thing is a trap. If only we knew exactly the amount of ice cream we could enjoy as a treat without gaining weight, we would not have to eliminate it from our diet. We all have a tendency to take the good thing and carry it too far. Aristotle tried to teach us about the Golden Mean of excellence between too little and too much, but, as a whole, few of us are wise enough to know when enough is enough.

We love the sun but after too much exposure we're told by our doctor we can no longer be out in the sun because it could cause cancer. We love wine, but if we drink too much it will become a trap. Think of coffee or chocolate or cookies. Our grandchildren look forward to their treats after supper. Their mother is wise to set strict limits on how much they're allowed in order to keep a treat a treat.

In the novel *Crime and Punishment*, the Russian writer Dostoyevsky pointed to the reality of our human condition: "Man grows used to everything, the scoundrel!" You eagerly anticipate your chocolate ice cream cone. Your expectations are high. One more scoop won't hurt you. Once you've doubled the amount of ice cream you enjoy, it is hard to go back to one lonely scoop.

Within a short period of time we get used to whatever we have. The novelty wears off and we begin to take good things for granted. Harvard psychologist Daniel Gilbert wrote a wise, witty book entitled *Stumbling on Happiness*. He asks the reader, Do you think you know what makes you happy? Perhaps not. Gilbert shakes us up about the foibles of our imagination.

Socrates understood: "What a lot of things there are a man can do without." We work hard, earn money, and we add good things, anticipating what will increase our happiness. We buy bigger houses, buy pretty things to fill them, and become collectors. With each added possession, we require more money to purchase it and to maintain it. Our possessions possess us.

We're in the land of plenty with all our beautiful things, but when we're not mindful of when enough is enough, we lose the Golden Mean of excellence between too little and too much. We become emotionally and spiritually deprived. The only good thing we need plenty of is wisdom. This is usually hard earned because of our inability to envision how we'll feel when all our material needs are met. The real problem is greed. There are enough resources for our real needs, but not enough for all that we *think* we need. There is a huge difference between our needs and our wants.

The ice cream cone doesn't taste as sumptuous after the treat becomes a regular trap. The new car is no longer new and the snappy newer model is now available at your car dealer. It is indeed a good thing to have a garden plot that gives you joy, but it will also steal your weekend time with your books, lover, and friends if it grows into multiple beds that need pruning, watering, weeding, and mulching. Having a garden to tend makes you less mobile. Owning a vintage second home near the ocean can be a good thing but if you end up spending all your time and resources maintaining it, replacing gutters and roofs, having to paint the exterior every three years because it is near the water, it becomes a trap. The more possessions we have, the less freedom we have. Managing the maintenance of excessive ownership can become an overwhelming trap.

Perhaps we become enlightened when we eliminate some good things, simplify the outward details of our lives, and allow ourselves greater freedom. We are at the banquet. We have enough. Our lasting happiness does not depend on anything that is seen by the eye but on what is felt in our hearts. Thomas Jefferson summed it up: "It is neither wealth nor splendor, but tranquility and occupation which give happiness." Keep in mind that your real needs are few and be careful what you wish for, because when you get what you think you want, it could seriously complicate your life and compromise your happiness for two.

IF THERE IS TO BE ANY PEACE
IT WILL COME THROUGH *BEING*,
NOT HAVING.

Henry Miller

50

Remember Important Dates

PRAY, LOVE, REMEMBER.

Shakespeare

Make a fuss over each other *every* day, but be sincerely sentimental on important dates.

Do you remember when, where, and how you met? When you were first in love, did you celebrate the first-month anniversary, the sixth month, the eighth month, and the tenth month? What music did you listen to on your first date? Let these markings be a cause to celebrate your love. Honoring important dates is a simple way to boost our happiness. Special occasions should indeed be special. Even if you don't enjoy growing older, recognizing your birth date is vitally important. And—yes—every Valentine's Day, we can remind each other how much we love each other.

I know a lot of dour people who can't bring themselves to write a love letter, wrap a present, or bring home flowers. It is as if they suffer from amnesia.

Discuss ahead of time how you want to celebrate important dates. All of us should pay attention to anniversaries of our love as well as our career. I was lecturing in Lexington, Kentucky, on March 9, 2007, the thirtieth anniversary of Alexandra Stoddard, Incorporated. I've always loved working on the anniversary of founding my company. This particular year I spoke about antiques at the Blue Grass Trust Garden and Antiques Show in the morning and in the afternoon I gave a talk on "Creating a Happy Home." Peter saw some glorious gigantic white oriental lilies and bought me several stems to celebrate this important date. I was photographed holding the lilies; I enjoyed having them in the hotel room and can recall their perfume and their glory.

Important dates are just that: important. When we remember and commemorate them, we're sharing happiness for two.

THE GREATEST TRAGEDY
IS INDIFFERENCE.

Red Cross Motto

51

Women Like to Talk Things Out

HE WAS NOT READY TO RECEIVE
WHAT I HAD TO BRING.

Simone de Beauvoir

I believe that overall, men and women are more alike than different, but women, as a general rule, like to talk about their feelings. They like to relate. The American anthropologist Margaret Mead believed women have an age-old training in human relations "for that is what feminine intuition really is—women have a special contribution to make to any group enterprise, and I feel it is up to them to contribute the kinds of awareness that relatively few men . . . have incorporated through their education."

Over many years Peter has come to understand that I like to talk things out, and not have him cut me off, dismissing me by saying, "You made your point." Peter doesn't intend to be dismissive, but he believes, as a trained trial lawyer, "When you've made your point, sit down."

I want to talk things out in hopes that my true love will become more emotionally available to my situation. I was on book tour in Milwaukee when I learned that the great racehorse Barbaro had died. I was crying when Peter came down the stairs to join me in the lobby of a club where we were staying. "What's wrong?" "Barbaro died," I answered, sobbing a little. Peter patted me and said he was sorry.

Flying home later in the day, I wanted to talk about Barbaro. For me, communicating my emotions to a loved one helps me to heal. It was awkward because Peter hates to see me sad; but when I made him aware that I needed to talk things out, he was able to listen and I was able to smile and wipe away my tears. When we're in close propinquity with our partners, we both like to talk and we discuss things on different levels. Celebrate your differences by keeping the line of communication flowing. Lovers should never feel lonely when they're alone, together when they can be heard, loved, and understood.

I have great respect for the "male" style of expressing emotions. While I tend to think out loud, Peter often wants to talk less about his feelings. We've learned how to communicate, perhaps not always with words. I respect his need to be silent or just hold hands. I can hug him and "relate" in *his* way.

Our feelings, when communicated, awaken and nourish our soul, helping us understand intangible mysteries. There's an ancient Hindu saying, "When the mind empties, the heart fills in." Illumination for two awaits when we communicate from the heart.

WOMEN CAN'T HAVE AN HONEST
EXCHANGE IN FRONT OF MEN
WITHOUT HAVING IT CALLED A
CAT FIGHT.

Clare Boothe Luce

52

Don't Correct Each Other in Public

OH, YES, I REMEMBER IT WELL.

Maurice Chevalier

When you are out with a group of people, it is a wise habit not to correct your partner in front of others. Each of you should feel free to enter into conversation, tell interesting stories and jokes, and not feel someone is waiting to correct an error, however slight, in memory.

Don't be so literal. No one should feel constrained in conversation with others. There's no reason to avoid some exaggeration or embellishment if that is someone's current spirit. Being matter-of-fact can be dull and unimaginative. The poet Emily Dickinson liked to say we should tell the truth, but tell it "slant." We're all entitled to present ourselves in a way that conforms with our particular viewpoint.

It really takes the wind out of someone's sails when you chime in and correct an error. Take a deep breath. Ask yourself, does this really matter?

Let your partner have free rein. I'd prefer it if Peter didn't make political toasts or jokes in public but I go along with it because he is enjoying himself and gets some laughs. He tends to exaggerate the punch line and one or two literal-minded people catch him on it and say, "That could never have happened." "That's okay," Peter says.

It is not our job to "make over" our soul mate. It is especially inappropriate to be critical in public. When we are alone we're frank and may challenge something one of us says: "Do you really think that?" But when we are with others we should try not to correct each other. Peter will set me up to tell a story and I often say, "You tell it, Peter." When he does, it isn't exactly the story, line by line, I would have told, but what difference does it make?

If your partner tells a joke, don't laugh before the punch line, or worse, give it before he or she does. Obviously there will be some jokes you've heard before. So what?

We can also remind each other of the names and some personal information about the people we're with in order to avoid a faux pas. Who among us can cast the first stone?

Allow each other to be more playful in social settings and be as supportive as possible of the way your lover expresses himself or herself in public.

CRITICISM IS EASY;
ART IS DIFFICULT.
Philippe Nericault

53

Generous Compliments Lighten the Heart

THE DEEPEST PRINCIPLE
IN HUMAN NATURE
IS THE CRAVING TO BE
APPRECIATED.

William James

When we're generous with our compliments we're expressing our praise, affection, and admiration. We send our good wishes. We all want to be loved, understood, and appreciated. Compliments reinforce our excellent qualities.

Many times I'll intuitively give someone a genuine compliment, then learn that what I said was just what that person needed to hear. It makes me happy to have been able to make an observation that made a difference to someone's sense of well-being. The doctor and author Deepak Chopra teaches us, "Dwell upon what is most lovable about the person who is most loving in your life today." Through thinking the thoughts that will recall the greatness and grace in our lover, as well as attentive observation, we can sing the praises of our lover. Lord Byron recognized, "Who loves, raves."

Human beings are motivated by praise; show your sincere approval and admiration. Our lover is praiseworthy: Rave! Establish the habit of lightening hearts with genuine generous compliments. Does it come easily to you to compliment others? The more we sincerely compliment people, the more we build our own confidence in our capacity to give pleasure to others. I'm used to Peter complimenting me often. I don't, as a rule, have to fish for a compliment. But when I feel attractively dressed and my spirits are high, I might inquire with a smile, "How do I look?"

Be unending in your generosity of spirit. The more often we are given a compliment, the more we feel we're on our path, recognized for what we do well. Think of all the creative compliments—praising tangible as well as intangible qualities—you can pay to your partner. Be specific.

- I love the tie and shirt combination you're wearing today.
- I've never known you to be more understanding or flexible than you were this afternoon.
- You write the most magnificent letters.
- Your toast at the dinner party this evening was brilliant.
- You make everyone feel so relaxed.
- You've never looked more rested or happy.
- Your smile makes me melt.
- You make me feel so loved and appreciated.
- I admire the way you handled such a sensitive situation.
- Whenever we dance, you make me feel graceful and beautiful.
- I admire your generosity and kindness toward everyone you know.

Let others criticize. Honest compliments are the language of love. When we praise our significant other we lift each other up into greater heights of happiness. Life and love take effort. Recognize it in each other and let your kind words melt your lover's heart.

KIND WORDS PRODUCE THEIR OWN IMAGE
IN MEN'S SOULS, AND A BEAUTIFUL IMAGE
IT IS. THEY SOOTHE AND QUIET AND
COMFORT THE HEARER . . .
WE HAVE NOT YET BEGUN TO USE KIND WORDS
IN SUCH ABUNDANCE AS THEY OUGHT TO BE USED.

Blaise Pascal

54

Explore Together Your Invisible Wealth

LIFE IS A PURE FLAME, AND
WE LIVE BY AN INVISIBLE
SUN WITHIN US.

Thomas Browne

When I lecture, I'm fond of quoting one of my favorite writers, the German poet Rainer Maria Rilke, who, in *Letters to a Young Poet*, wrote: "If your daily life seems poor, do not blame it, blame yourself for you are not poet enough to call forth its riches." We should value our mutual inner resources that build the foundation of our lasting happiness for two.

A Wall Street mogul was in Florence, Italy, with his wife and she was surprised by joy as she experienced the divine light of the sunset over the Arno River. When she told her husband to look at this splendor, he grumbled, "I can't buy it or sell it, come on, we're late for the restaurant."

A wealthy Texas widow came to New York to buy some French Impressionist art. I met her for breakfast at the Carlyle Hotel to discuss plans for the day. When I told her about the Claude Monet exhibition at the Metropolitan Museum of Art just a few blocks away, I admitted, "I've been to see these splendid paintings every morning since this exhibit opened. I think this would be such an excellent way to train our eye." Harriett looked at me with a puzzled expression. "Alexandra, I'm here to buy art, not look at art. I can't buy anything at a museum. Let's go to the galleries on your list." And that's exactly what we did.

While there are many beautiful material riches, the greatest ones are in our mind. We're born with an underdeveloped mind that we inherited, but the ultimate mind is one we develop, and the greatest inner resource we will ever possess. Someone once said that it is better to strengthen your back than to lighten your burden. Our mind needs to be exercised and our soul needs to be nourished. Our soul informs us of divine ideals, our heart is our treasure, and our mind tells us of things visible and invisible. When we think about our invisible wealth we are prosperous indeed, valuing our real treasures of love, satisfaction, inner peace, wisdom, virtue, compassion, patience, and a joyful spirit.

From one to ten, how content do you believe you are? No matter how materially wealthy you are, if you are discontented you are poor in spirit.

The Chinese Taoist philosopher Lao Tzu, born around 600 B.C., believed there were five blessings—health, wealth, happiness, longevity, and peace. Together, let's explore our invisible wealth. The icon of the American left, the linguist Noam Chomsky, thought "we should look at ourselves through our own eyes and not other people's eyes." When we are grateful for all of our blessings, we are abundantly rich. Cicero taught "gratitude is not only the greatest of virtues, but the parent of all the others."

We've all been brought up to appreciate material things. I've spent my career dealing in beautiful man-made objects. Some people are more acquisitive than others, more eager to possess. On a scale of one to ten, how acquisitive do you think you are? Have you tended to become more so, or do you find you have less need to own so many beautiful things, relying more on your invisible wealth? If we spend all our energies acquiring material objects, we tend to overlook or ignore the most essential things that can't be seen or touched.

Below is a list of some of the invisible wealth you can explore together to increase your happiness for two. Add your own to this list:

reputation

charity

soul

character

spirit

optimism

happiness

laughter

health

charm

meditation

enthusiasm

conscience

joy

friendship

gratitude

intuition

altruism

freedom

prayer

faith

energy

wonderful memories

hope

reading

laughter
love
writing
learning
desire
dreams

You and your love are surrounded by invisible wealth. You live in a perpetual state of blessings. You can go to the free library to read and learn together. You can visit an art gallery to experience beautiful, inspiring art together. You can walk about and enjoy the beauty and proportions of fine architecture together. You can walk and swim at a public beach together. You can climb a mountain and campout together. You can love each other wherever you are.

Dwell in the elevated consciousness of your collective invisible wealth.

IT IS ONLY WITH THE HEART THAT ONE CAN
SEE RIGHTLY; WHAT IS ESSENTIAL IS INVISIBLE
TO THE EYE.

Antoine de Saint-Exupery

55

Don't Discuss Weight

A CRUST EATEN IN PEACE
IS BETTER THAN A BANQUET
PARTAKEN IN ANXIETY.

Aesop

I love good food. I'm grateful that I have a huge appetite for life. Food is a necessary pleasure I indulge in with great relish three times a day. Whatever I eat, I try to do so mindfully, attuned to my body's needs. A thoughtful nutritious diet, regular exercise, fresh air, and ample sleep can do wonders to prevent illness. A wise Buddhist proverb makes sense: "Eat when you're hungry. Drink when you're thirsty. Sleep when you're tired."

Meals are to be savored; they are opportunities for happiness for two. The twentieth-century British writer and critic C. S. Lewis remarked: "The sun looks down on nothing half as good as a household laughing together over a meal." Peter and I enjoy our meals, appreciating every flavor; we eat slowly and stop before we are full, letting ourselves find real satisfaction.

Try not to bring up the delicate subject of weight. All of us are aware of our weight. Those of us who don't weigh ourselves know how loose or tight our clothes are. We should be conscious, not self-conscious, about our weight. It is never appropriate to discuss someone else's weight. We all know what we put in our mouth. Our weight will fluctuate, but it is no one's business but our own.

There are a few simple disciplines I've made into habits. I try not to eat standing up. I try not to snack or nibble. I order small portions of a variety of foods when I'm at a restaurant because I have a bad habit of eating everything that is served to me—a throwback to "the Clean Plate Club" of my childhood: We were rewarded when we cleaned our plate and punished when we didn't.

To slow down my eating and therefore feel full on less food, I use chopsticks. My weight is my business, and I've chosen not to make it a problem. If your partner orders french fries and asks you if you want some, simply say "no thanks." If your love wants to share a dessert with you, have one taste. If your lover is not as disciplined as you are, set a good example and don't discuss weight!

THE DISCOVERY OF A NEW DISH
DOES MORE FOR HUMAN HAPPINESS THAN
THE DISCOVERY OF A NEW STAR.

Anthelme Brillat-Savarin

56

Try Not to Interrupt

TO SEIZE THE FLYING THOUGHT
BEFORE IT ESCAPES US IS OUR
ONLY TOUCH WITH REALITY.

Ellen Glasgow

When you interrupt someone, you can cause damage to ideas in formation. There are times when we need to concentrate without distractions. I confess I interrupt Peter a great deal and am making an effort to be more thoughtful. Because Peter and I are always together, there are ample opportunities and excuses to interrupt. Sometimes I ask Peter a question from another room, not even aware he's on the telephone. It is counterproductive and rude, really. When necessary, Peter tunes out in self-defense in order to maintain inner peace and to think clearly. We've established a policy that is useful. We announce in advance when we are not verbally available to each other, when we're on the phone, writing, or studying and wish not to be disturbed.

A couple we know had to readjust their habits when Joe decided to start his own company and work from home. Vicki was glad to have him around during the day and developed the habit of interrupting Joe.

Joe explained to Vicki that he needed more continuity of thought, and the constant interruptions of his concentration were frustrating. Vicki understood. She became her own cheerleader. Rather than asking Joe for advice, she'd work things out on her own. When she figured something out by herself, she'd say, "Hey, Vicki!" Yes. It was working.

Out of consideration we should refrain from petty interruptions. I can check the spelling of a word in the dictionary rather than being lazy and asking Peter. I try to speak to Peter only when I'm in the same room. I also try to be sensitive to his body language to sense when he is in need of quiet. We both announce when we need time with no interruptions. In this way, one of us can answer the door or the house phone to cover for our partner. The telephone is not answered when we're both focused on mental work.

If we think of something we want to discuss or ask the other, we can make a note and discuss it when it's mutually convenient, providing quiet space for the muse. Timing is key. Protect each other's solitude.

INTERRUPTION IS UNWELCOME.

PLEASE NOT NOW.

Anonymous

57

Tit-for-Tat Is Tiresome

IF LOVE DOES NOT KNOW HOW
TO GIVE AND TAKE WITHOUT
RESTRICTIONS, IT IS NOT LOVE,
BUT A TRANSACTION THAT
NEVER FAILS TO LAY STRESS
ON A PLUS AND A MINUS.

Emma Goldman

When we love someone completely, we don't keep score. We try to go the extra mile with grace. Children tat when someone tits—they fight back. As adults we come to understand that life is not always fair, or "even-Steven." There are reasons for some things to happen the way they do and these should not be questioned.

If someone does something that is inconvenient or frustrating, it should never be countered by a payback and a "so there!" We want things to be fair and equal but, as we know from experience, things will never be perfectly balanced. Couples work out the different ways they can help each other. In most love relationships, one partner does more of the domestic work than the other. Child care and responsibility falls on the shoulders of one person more than the other, especially during the week. If possible, it seems fair for a spouse or partner to gladly take care of the children for a few hours to free up time for a yoga class or time to have a haircut without demanding equal time off to go swimming or go to the gym, unless that is the "happiness boost" encouraged by their love.

Not keeping score should apply to all aspects of your life together. If one set of parents lives much closer than the other, you will probably be spending more time with them. Think of having quality time with others, not quantity. We work things out as best we can. When circumstances change, we may need to rethink everything. If someone goes back to school to work toward a graduate degree, the other partner will temporarily carry a greater financial load as well as cover more of the maintenance day to day.

Everything has or should have a way of working out over the long haul. Keep the big picture in mind. We give what we have. Our finances are rarely even. If one has more and the other has less, "Your turn to treat; my turn to treat" is often unfair. And if you do, you could sadly play tit-for-tat indefinitely. If your partner loves to cook, let him cook for you. You do household chores and take the lion's share of the responsibility for the children. The secret is to stop comparing and live your life as fairly and as lovingly as possible.

Generously give to your love. Think of how you can add to your mutual equanimity, where there is a calm, cheerful atmosphere, both partners feeling appreciated and adored. Yes, tit-for-tat is tiresome.

IT IS A DISASTER TO HAVE A
MAN FALL IN LOVE WITH ME. THEY AREN'T
CONTENT TO TAKE WHAT I CAN GIVE,
THEY WANT EVERYTHING FROM ME.

Katherine Anne Porter

58

Conversations Shouldn't Be Monologues

WHEN A CONVERSATION BECOMES A
MONOLOGUE, POKED ALONG WITH TINY
CATTLE PROD QUESTIONS, IT ISN'T A
CONVERSATION ANYMORE.

Barbara Walters

There are times to listen and there are times to talk. When partners are together, one should not be engaged in a soliloquy where one character reveals his or her thoughts unaware of the presence of others. When two are together, one is not speaking to oneself. There should be a rhythm, a desire for conversation, a meeting of hearts and minds. This informal exchange should not be monopolized by one person but should be an interchange.

Love requires interaction. When we're able to give and receive reciprocally, we're both fully engaged. Have you ever been at a restaurant and overheard one person doing all the talking during the entire evening? The other people suffocate as they nod without a break.

I have the bad habit of interrupting. When I'm engaged in stimulating conversation, my mind jumps in and my mouth opens. I become enthusiastic and want to add something relevant, afraid if I don't chime in, I'll miss the muse. But this goes both ways: If I don't let the person finish his thought, he could forget what he was saying. Often Peter will say, "Let me finish," when I don't wait through a pause.

Conversation is one of the greatest ways of experiencing happiness when people come together to share their thoughts, insights, and feelings. No one should feel rushed or have to talk fast; we should be relaxed and at leisure when we're in conversation.

Whatever you're talking about, inquire what someone wants to add to the experience. There is an art to questioning in order to bring out the other person's self-expression. If you're talking, you can use some inviting phrases to encourage others to express their point of view:

"Have you felt that way?"

"What do you think?"

"Do you remember?"

"What has been your experience?"

"Do you tend to look to the future more than the past?"

Once we open up the conversation to taking in the stories and insights of others, we enhance our own thinking and increase our shared experiences and humanity. I always enjoy interchange after giving a lecture, glad the discussion isn't limited to questions and answers.

When conversations are free of monologues, we're able to affirm and confirm what we hear, as well as adding to our body of anecdote and inspiration. Face-to-face conversation can often be illuminating and electrifying. Everyone present should be encouraged to participate by speaking up. Conversation is not a speech. We all have the floor.

TWO HEADS ARE BETTER THAN ONE.

John Heywood

59

Be More Sentimental and Indulge Each Other

TENDERNESS . . . THE JOY OF BEING
FRIENDLY, OF BEING WARM, OF
CONSIDERING AND RESPECTING
ANOTHER PERSON AND OF MAKING
THIS OTHER PERSON HAPPY.

Erich Fromm

Peter and I are enthusiastic romantics. We are sentimental and indulge each other with great regularity. We're imaginative, not practical. Our romantic natures keep the flame of love alive. Our sentiments bring us closer because our thoughts and attitude are based more on emotion than reason. We're easily given to thoughts and feelings of love. We still woo each other after all these years. We're still on our honeymoon; we fell in love and have pampered each other ever since.

I remember when we were first married, Peter's sisters frowned on our public displays of affection. To this day, we kiss in public and we always hold hands.

When I asked my readers what they most admired in their own character or in the character of others throughout history, a woman from Vero Beach, Florida, said, "I know how wonderful my husband is." We should continuously tell our love how much their presence means to us every day. She went on to say they have a beautiful life, four children and are more in love today than they were twenty-five years ago when they married.

On a scale of one to ten, how romantic are you? Is your partner sentimental? In a loving, caring relationship, we indulge each other's whims and desires. We adore going to musicals, the more romantic the better. I love *My Fair Lady* and was thrilled to go on my birthday when we went to the revival on Broadway. Peter and I got dressed up and he treated me to dinner at Café des Artistes after the theater. Go out of your way to let your partner know how much you care, in order not to let your love fall into indifference. The American poet Robert Frost wrote, "Love is an irresistible desire to be irresistibly desired." Because none of us ever feels enough love, Peter and I are in the habit of saying "I love you" whenever the spirit moves us, and that is often.

How do you indulge your partner? I was happy to read recently that 69 percent of men spent over $100 on their significant other last Valentine's Day. It's not the dollar amount but the fact that they wanted to be sentimental that matters. Of course, the point is that we should be more sentimental throughout the year. When we show our affection through indulgences, we honor our lover. Peter and I give each other useful, indulgent gifts. I love to buy him aftershave and neckties. He enjoys buying me perfume, cologne, and scented candles. These gifts we use and enjoy together every day:

- favorite bath gel
- a tiny flashlight to bring to a restaurant to read the menu
- a silk pocket square for a blazer
- a colorful silk change purse or key case
- sharp shears to cut flowers
- a box of pretty notecards
- colorful boxer shorts and socks

- a pair of wineglasses
- colorful floral paper napkins

There are endless ways we can love each other sensuously and keep a long, sentimental courtship alive. When we share sentiments we create "moments," the poet John Keats wrote, "big as years." Let your mutual love increase your vulnerability. Romance has no bounds. The more sentimental we are, the more lovable we become. The French fashion designer Coco Chanel was asked by a young lady where she was to use perfume. Chanel answered, "Wherever you want to be kissed." Oh yes, wouldn't *that* be loverly?

FILL YOUR LIFE WITH LOVE,
SCATTER SUNSHINE.

Norman Vincent Peale

60

Never Pick a Fight

IF WE ALLOW LOVE AND COMPASSION
TO BE DOMINATED BY ANGER, WE
WILL SACRIFICE THE BEST PART OF
OUR HUMAN INTELLIGENCE—WISDOM,
OUR ABILITY TO DECIDE BETWEEN RIGHT
AND WRONG. ALONG WITH SELFISHNESS,
ANGER IS ONE OF THE MOST SERIOUS
PROBLEMS FACING THE WORLD TODAY.

The Dalai Lama

Peter is a professional arguer because of his legal training as a federal prosecutor of organized crime and as a civil trial lawyer. I've had to remind him on several occasions that whatever the circumstances, no one wins a fight when love is there. Picking a fight causes you more trouble than the original conflict; therefore it is counterproductive and should be avoided. Picking a fight, deliberately provoking your partner by tone of voice, use of harsh words, and calling up past problems that were hurtful to both partners creates scars that last long after the dispute is over. Picking a fight can be a serious character flaw, even a sign of ignorance.

Happiness for two is a commitment we make together to love each other unconditionally. Peter and I set our minds and hearts not to fight. If we ever feel in the least bit upset with each other we try to look inward, examining our own conscience to bring out more love, compassion, and empathy. How many of us can honestly say we have our anger in check when we pick a fight?

It is never appropriate to be preemptive or aggressive. When anyone picks a fight by pressing someone's buttons, they may be sabotaging the partnership. Wise people will never be the saboteur because it is a destruction of the commitment to love each other. When we have a strong desire to live the good life, we must take the high road, not get swept down to lowlife, combative behavior. If you are tempted to quarrel or to pick a fight out of anger or frustration, walk away. Some people are pugnacious and have a ready inclination to fight. (I laugh when I learn from studies on happiness that lawyers tend to be among the least happy people.) One thing leads to another, and too often cutting words lead to violent behavior. Argumentative people can destroy lives. Accounts of domestic violence are sad reports in our daily news.

Try not to dwell on old, bitter grievances when you are out of sorts and are provoked and resentful. Any negative feelings that stir you to action will result in bad behavior. I'll never forget a woman who walked into one of my book signings on a snowy, freezing evening. Her eyes were red and she was visibly upset when she joined the group listening to my talk. She stood in the back, and later told me she had come to the store to browse and calm down after a dreadful fight with her husband. She said she couldn't wait to go home to kiss and make up and apologize for the fight.

Even if you are blessed with a blissful relationship, you could be in a feud with a relative or in-law that is extremely painful and hard to reconcile. Remain calm, go about your life and, if confronted, attempt to placate or come to a realistic compromise. It is better to grant concessions than to become angry. Fighting makes it difficult to reestablish closeness in a love relationship. Helen Keller once said that she never fought except against difficulties.

Regularly, lovingly, discuss the situations that are most troublesome with your partner. Immediately recognize what you're getting into and where the discussion has deteriorated in the past. Call upon your sense of compassion for the ongoing points of tension about the conflicts between you.

The Golden Rule of Taoism is to recompense injury with kindness. Saint Francis taught that where there is injury, pardon. Whenever we refuse to fight, we eliminate a major source of suffering. Peace be with you.

BLESSED ARE THE PEACEMAKERS
ON EARTH.

Shakespeare

61

Please Don't Say Something You'll Regret

NO ONE IS SUCH A LIAR
AS THE INDIGNANT MAN.

Nietzsche

When two people come together in love, they share a great deal of conversation, mostly intimate. There is much more opportunity to say something you'll regret, to say what you feel in the heat of the moment. This relationship is not just a date, a pleasant night out, but a vital lifetime experience. What could possibly be more intimate and personal?

When awkward, unpleasant situations come up, we need to choose our words with greater care in this most powerful of relationships. When we deviate from this thoughtfulness, we can cause deep wounds. Some people who have been badly hurt never forget.

If we belittle others, we diminish ourselves. Those sad souls who do can expect to be lonely. The ancient Greek biographer and philosopher Plutarch advised, "It is wise to be silent when occasion requires." The Dalai Lama believes there are times to adopt a dignified silence.

Whenever you become frustrated, goaded, and at your wits' end, please don't say something you'll regret. We're all leaflike fragile. A rift you cause because of your words can take some time to heal. For example, if your lover has had too much to drink at a party, you might lovingly suggest it is time to go home, to bed. But if you accuse your significant other of being a drunk, this leaves scar tissue that doesn't go away.

If your loved one has a child from another relationship, it is best not to criticize. You may feel you've never known anyone more obnoxious than your lover's son or daughter, but it is wise to keep this to yourself.

People's words can be bombs, and the closer your partnership, the more explosive words can be. Peter was a trial lawyer for fifty-five years and, whenever we engaged in an argument, he'd say, "Strike it from the record." From my experience, no one can ever strike anything from the record. We tend to dwell on the insults and remember them. Some wise noble souls can forgive, but I believe only enlightened people are able to forgive and forget.

I can still recall, after fifty years, someone I cared deeply about telling me I had no sense of humor. It was such a powerful blow that I felt as if I never wanted to say another word to that person.

Whenever someone picks on another person, it is always a reflection of themselves. If someone deliberately tries to hurt your feelings, *they* are obviously hurting. Let's, together, try to live lovingly and try not to say anything we'll be sorry about later.

HEAR NO EVIL, SEE NO EVIL,
SPEAK NO EVIL.
**Three wise monkeys,
carved over door of sacred stable,
Nikko, Japan**

62

Play to Each Other's Strengths

EACH CITIZEN SHOULD PLAY
HIS PART IN THE COMMUNITY
ACCORDING TO HIS INDIVIDUAL GIFTS.

Plato

E ach of us has certain abilities, skills, and talents that lighten the load of whatever work we're doing. When we emphasize our strong points, we'll find more pleasure and ease in whatever we do. In a partnership, each person pulls their own weight by contributing to the relationship what they're good at. We're all, in some way, gifted, endowed with great natural ability and intelligence. We can't assume our partner has the same capacity or inclination as we do. The formula for happiness for two is that each person pursues his own passions and the other one benefits from the fruits.

Whenever we play to each other's strengths we accomplish our goals effectively, resisting stress or strain. If one of you loves to decorate, cook, and arrange flowers, the other might be one who enjoys fixing things, making sure everything around the house is in working order. One of you loves to drive and the other loves to be driven. One of you enjoys handling the correspondence and the other thrives nurturing the children and grandchildren. If you're born with a green thumb, use this gift to create a wonderful garden for everyone to feel the beauty and experience the peacefulness. If one person enjoys researching future travel opportunities, the other one can be playing the piano, sweetening the atmosphere of the home.

We find our happiness for two on our own terms, revealing to each other the talents and abilities we have that bring richness and stimulation to both of our lives in equal measure. You may excel at putting together the tax information for the accountant and your other half is better at calming and nursing a feverish child. One of you can patiently cut through red tape; one can make quick friends. You may be verbal and your partner is visual. If you are musical, your mate may be logical. We're better off when we gladly do what comes naturally to us and share these gifts with our partner.

HE FLOURISHES IN HIS STRENGTH.

Homer

63

Set Aside Certain Times for Serious Discussions

TALKING IS LIKE PLAYING ON THE HARP;
THERE IS AS MUCH IN LAYING THE
HANDS ON THE STRINGS TO STOP
THEIR VIBRATION AS IN TWANGING
THEM TO BRING OUT THEIR MUSIC.

Oliver Wendell Holmes

There are times in all loving relationships when you will have conversations that are serious, where life changes will transpire. Timing is critical. Rather than randomly falling into these defining times, it is wise to set the stage where you can make a date ahead of time to talk things through.

Be in a receptive mood. When you're both open to new ways to improve your happiness, this is a great opportunity to share ideas in a loving way. Select a comfortable place to have your talk. Try to have total privacy where you both can feel unconstrained and can hear each other. Give each other your undivided attention. Often Peter and I have serious discussions when we're traveling. Somehow travel makes us feel expansive and receptive to change. It seems natural to talk when you're away from children, work, and domestic distractions. Peter and I were in Florida on vacation several years ago when our serious discussion led us to put our house on the market.

Both of you will speak from your heart, but be prepared. Gather your thoughts ahead of time and make a few notes. You want to think of the whole picture. Whenever we change one thing, everything else has to be reconsidered. Voice your thoughts from your own point of view, while also considering your partner's needs and desires in a spirit of openness.

No matter how many different topics you cover, there should be a meeting of the minds as you tenderly explore ways to improve your lives together. No one else will ever understand why you do or don't do certain things. Feel grateful you have each other's well-being as your top priority. With that as the focus, everything else will fall into place nicely. Sensitive communication is the wisest way for two lovers to seek and find lasting unity. The more times you set aside to discuss serious matters, the more loved you will feel and the more lovable you'll be. Two people will understand. That is all you need to move forward with confidence and harmony.

WE TALK LITTLE, IF WE DO
NOT TALK ABOUT OURSELVES.
William Hazlitt

Control Your Tone

THAT LOVELY VOICE, HOW
I SHOULD WEEP FOR JOY
IF I COULD HEAR IT NOW!

Colette

One of the most beautiful things one can offer to another is a gentle and melodious voice. Your vocal tone defines you. You can tell a great deal about someone's personality by their tone of voice—it is perhaps one of the most significant attributes a person can have. Our voice is a distinctive feature of who we are and how we feel about ourselves and the world around us.

Each of us has a certain natural manner of expression that creates an atmosphere that can be either pleasant or harsh. It is not always what you say but how you say it that counts. A tone of voice can express sarcasm, joy, cynicism, or anger. A simple "good-bye" said in an angry tone can cut you to the quick with pain. And one word, spoken sweetly in unqualified love, sounds truly good to the ear and lifts the spirit.

Soft, sweet tones coming from one loved one to another are powerful. The Spanish writer Cervantes, best known for his book *Don Quixote*, wrote, "Fair and softly goes far." Sweet voices seduce, opening us to be more intimate, romantic, and loving.

Although we all know some women who are so soft-spoken that no one can hear what they have to say, generally women have higher, more penetrating voice tones than men. Have you ever been to a restaurant with a group of women celebrating a birthday or baby shower? Women's voices tend to rise like flights of birds. Many men are not amused.

Many of us have no idea how our voice affects others. I often think we might record our voice to hear how we sound. If someone were to do an audio of you when you're frustrated or upset, you'd be surprised how harsh and unpleasant your voice tone can sound.

We should also consider volume and pronunciation as well as voice tone. I know many people who don't want to keep saying "What?" and consequently pretend that they have heard and understood when, in fact, that is not always true. There are many people who are vain about their hearing. If your partner is hard of hearing and doesn't wear a hearing aid, be sure you enunciate your words clearly and move your mouth in order for your love to read your lips as well as hear your voice.

Take some deep breaths before you speak when you feel harassed, frustrated, or overwhelmed. If you don't wish to irritate or exhaust love, control your tone. Gentle voices are the melody of true love.

SPEAK LOW, IF YOU SPEAK LOVE.

Shakespeare

65

Grumpiness Is Contagious

BE CHEERFUL WHILE YOU
ARE ALIVE.

Ptahhotpe

D o you consider your natural disposition to be good-natured? When we're in good spirits, we bless everyone around us. A cheerful soul promotes cheer, encouraging others to become happier. Emerson figured out that "good-nature is stronger than tomahawks." A genuinely positive disposition is powerful. When in good spirits, we are an example to others. We do tend to model our behavior after that of the people we are with. Think of your cheerfulness as ripples in a pond scattering rays of sunlight in all directions. When we have an easygoing, cheerful attitude, we spread goodness everywhere we go.

At a bookstore talk in Milwaukee, I said, "Happiness is our choice." A man raised his hand and said, "Mrs. Stoddard, I'm a curmudgeon. I'm a mean, nasty, cantankerous person, and I'm happy being grumpy." Everyone laughed and some people even clapped. His wife waited in line to have me autograph her book. Her husband was grumbling about the long wait. "Let's go home; you don't need her autograph." This patient wife whispered to me, "Fifty-four years and I haven't been able to change him. He's actually more grumpy in his old age than ever."

This husband's disparaging remarks belittled his wife. I felt sorry for this saint who put up with him and breathed a sigh of relief that I didn't have to go home and live with his toxic energy. The toxicity of grumpiness is poisonous in an intimate relationship and destroys any hope for mutual happiness or transformation.

An anonymous writer once put it, "Be a fountain, not a drain." Grumpy people take the wind out of our sails. Who among us would wish to be with a cranky, complaining partner? A grumpy soul deeply affects the life force of his lover.

Grumpiness unfortunately is contagious. Daniel Goleman teaches us in *Social Intelligence* that we mirror the bad behavior of someone we're with. Negative energy tends to spread. While it is wise, whenever possible, for the sake of our health, to avoid people who are chronically grumpy, when we're in a committed relationship, what can we do? In order to save the situation and bolster the goal of happiness for two, there must be a confrontation where you lovingly explain that this behavior is unacceptable. When there is love for each other we assume responsibility. There needs to be reform in this precarious situation. Grumpiness must be faced head-on in order to improve the quality of the relationship and lead to greater well-being for both of you.

Be acutely aware of your own behavior when you are not at your best as well as when your partner is grumpy. This attitude of mind and heart is not normal or healthy and must be corrected each time it occurs. Mindfully face up to the inner workings of your heart. Spend some time alone to clear your head of negative thoughts that cause discomfort. Stay focused on your goal to be happy together.

If your partner is grumpy, gently, lovingly, say, "I love you." Don't get caught up and lose your cheerfulness. Together discuss the need to build each other up, keeping your mutual vow to be happy together.

I wish I had a magic wand and could miraculously make the grump cheer up. But, alas, no one can change another person, as we may have learned the hard way. "Ungrump." "Ungrump." It doesn't work. There is only one way for someone to transform their disposition and that is for them to realize that their negative temperament is hurtful, unloving, and dangerous to themselves as well as to their partner.

THE MIND IS ITS OWN
PLACE, AND IN ITSELF
CAN MAKE A HEAVEN OF HELL
OR HELL OF HEAVEN.

John Milton

Say "It's Okay"

WE FORGIVE SO LONG AS WE LOVE.

La Rochefoucauld

We often make mistakes, so we should be quick to give our partner a break and let him off the hook. Certainly there are times when our partner does something that could cause harm and we can't overlook it, but on the smaller offenses, say "It's okay" and move on.

Saint Francis of Assisi, who founded the Franciscan order in the early thirteenth century, taught us, "It is in pardoning that we are pardoned." Mother Teresa remarked, "If you judge people, you have no time to love them." When we are able to forgive, we are strong, understanding, and brave. We can learn to forgive many things, especially ourselves. If we can't forgive ourselves, who can?

Rise above the endless little things. Be quick to forgive your love. Kiss and make up. Don't waste time; value it and move on in order not to cause unnecessary pain to each other. Some people have a critical, perfectionistic disposition and they pick, pick, pick. But even someone with this nature can change and develop the habit of forgiving.

It is to *our* advantage to turn the other cheek because when we forgive others, we are happier. We relieve our mind of worries when we're able to move on. Value forgiveness as one of the keystones to your happiness for two. The French philosopher Voltaire's favorite maxim was "Love truth, but pardon error."

Forgiveness frees us, costs us nothing, and is the trademark of a noble soul. Whenever we have the inclination to blame others, we should examine ourselves. We are blessed to be in the company of a generous-spirited person who loves us as we are and who focuses on all that is positive and good about us.

Don't distress yourself with anything that will interfere with love in action. Let the Golden Rule enlarge your spirit as you say, "It's okay."

> SHE HUGG'D THE OFFENDER,
> AND FORGAVE THE OFFENSE.
>
> **John Dryden**

Patience, Patience

DELAY IS PREFERABLE TO ERROR.

Thomas Jefferson

P atience is an overlooked virtue, but it really is the sign of highly developed intelligence and wisdom. There is no way we can seek and find happiness for two without valuing our patience and being compassionately patient with our partner.

There is nothing quick or easy that is deeply meaningful or serious. Our amazing brains were made for finer things than to skim the surface superficially, racing from one task to another, running away from our center. If we choose to get caught up in the daily rat race, we have only ourselves to blame. Keep in mind the beautiful words of Eleanor McMillen Brown, my mentor, boss, and friend, who was born in 1890 and died five days before her one-hundred-and-first birthday. At the fine interior decorating firm she founded in 1924, Mrs. Brown taught her designers: "Create beauty for ourselves and create beauty for others, and you will live a long, happy life."

Mrs. Brown never let her clients rush the creative process. Once, when a notoriously difficult client tried to force her to come up with an immediate floor plan and scheme for his New York City apartment ballroom that seated two hundred people, she paused, and calmly said, "I don't know what the design will be; I haven't dreamed on it yet."

Patient people are not afraid to take their time to achieve greater inner peace and more clarity of mind. Patient people let others take their time. Patient people understand that living takes time. Face a hardship with patience and confidence that the issues can be resolved in good order, in due time. This positive attitude and approach avoids denial, panic, or despair.

Patient people are able to endure pain and difficulty with calmness, tolerance, and understanding. When persevering we're capable of awaiting an outcome without haste or being impulsive. We make better decisions. When necessary, we're able to suffer patiently without yielding. Patience is not entirely congenial to the American spirit. But couples should never underestimate the power of the passage of time and the wisdom of not necessarily requiring an instant resolution for whatever comes up.

Let life evolve. True patience is more than not being impatient. Patience is the beginning of wisdom.

PATIENCE IS THE BEST MEDICINE.

John Florio

68

Discover and Rediscover Each Other's Passions

THE ART OF LIVING DOES NOT CONSIST
IN PRESERVING AND CLINGING TO A
PARTICULAR HAPPINESS, BUT IN
ALLOWING HAPPINESS TO CHANGE
ITS FORM WITHOUT BEING DISAPPOINTED
BY THE CHANGE; FOR HAPPINESS,
LIKE A CHILD, MUST BE ALLOWED TO GROW UP.

Charles Langbridge Morgan

My spiritual guide and friend John Bowen Coburn taught me more than thirty years ago that we live our lives in chapters. The German writer, Goethe, said, "Each ten years of a man's life has its own fortunes, its own hopes, its own desires." The French fashion designer Yves Saint Laurent remarked that the most beautiful makeup of a woman is passion. What are you most passionate about now? What are some of the things that are most interesting to you? We should stay current with ourselves. We change from one day to the next. We're shedding the past we inherited as we make new discoveries. We're daring to truly be ourselves.

A forty-year-old woman confided in me at a book signing for *You Are Your Choices* that she was about to make a major change in her life. She said the book would help her. The only thing holding her back was that she knew her parents would disapprove. Sharon was petrified of their reaction. Unless we continuously discover and rediscover our own passions, however, we will not find fulfillment.

We need to encourage our partner to be true to the person he or she is *now,* not who they were, growing up under their parents' influence. We are learning to stretch ourselves to be the person we want to become. We are becoming the person we're meant to be. We need each other's encouragement, especially when parents or others don't understand or approve.

Human beings yearn for things to stay the same, but this is impossible. There is no permanence. Change is our constant reality from birth to death, and growing through change is our only hope for becoming wise. We're entirely different people now than we were when we were younger. Our character traits and personality may be consistent, but our lives evolve in mysterious ways, not much of it predictable.

Forty years ago, I discovered that many people I met were not happy in their houses; they were relying too heavily on their decorator or their friends to dictate a style for living their lives. I began to write about this. My first published book has the subtitle *How to Make Where You Live You.* I urged people to express themselves and be surrounded with objects they love. I wrote that people would run barefoot in a blizzard to be with you if you're happy at home.

One book led to another. I began to lecture and appear on television. My study of ancient Greek philosophy, pursued since my teenage years, led me to evolve into a lifestyle philosopher. Now, Peter and I are doing more traveling, lecturing, and writing than ever. He has become a nonpracticing counselor-at-law. We're enthusiastic about our adventure, not knowing exactly where we're going. We're now free to accept opportunities as they come to us.

What are some of the things that might ignite your passion? Think of the wide range of activities available to excite your curiosity, from crafts, dance, and the arts to volunteer charity activities and public service. Peter is passionate about travel, the theater, discovering bistros and brasseries. He is excited about learning more about international wines. Peter loves beauty in all forms and enjoys going to see great art around the world. We're both passionate about our young grandchildren, reading and writing, and each other. We're both hungry to learn, to grow, to explore and use as much of our potential as possible in the years ahead as we stay current with our passions. We know there will be lots of surprises. We embrace our unknown discoveries with boundless enthusiasm.

LOVE IS A KIND OF KNOWLEDGE OF
ANOTHER WHO IS IN ONE SENSE ONESELF.
THE KNOWLEDGE IS NEVER TOTAL, BUT IT IS QUITE
PERFECT IN ITS SPHERE.

Michael Drury

69

Eat as Many Meals Together as Possible

IT'S FUN TO GET TOGETHER AND
HAVE SOMETHING GOOD TO EAT
AT LEAST ONCE A DAY.
THAT'S WHAT HUMAN LIFE IS ALL
ABOUT—ENJOYING THINGS.

Julia Child

Since the beginning of time, bonding conversations, exchanging information and inspiration as well as romance, have happened over food. When two people like each other, they'll desire to break bread together. Whenever Peter and I enjoy a meal together, whether at home or at a restaurant, we are on a date. It is a treat to be able to talk privately about what is on our minds and in our hearts.

We try to allow plenty of time in order not to rush. Over a delicious meal, we're able to unwind, completely relax into the moment, talk, plan, and rejoice. Food is one of my ten defining words. I love to tell people, laughing, "I've never missed a meal."

As Julia Child said, we're meant to enjoy our lives and food plays an important part in a pleasant, happy life. The more meals you can share together, the better. Certainly you should have at least one meal a day with your partner without the television.

Eating meals together is civilized, something we can plan ahead of time and arrange as a priority in order to keep our intimacy. If both partners are working, the elegant, home-cooked dinner may not appear on the table, but even if it is takeout from the Chinese or Thai place you love, or something ordered in, the point is to be together and focused on each other. Your meals don't have to be highly planned or fancy—you can pick up a roasted chicken from the market, some French bread, rice, and a fresh vegetable, open a bottle of wine, light some candles, set the table with colorful paper napkins, and voilà!

Whether you go out for breakfast on Saturdays or have a special ritual at home with omelets and muffins or you regularly go out to brunch on Sundays, the more dates you make to share meals together, the more you'll stay connected.

When you're eating supper at home, take an extra two minutes to change out of your business clothes and put on a fresh shirt. Create a sensuous atmosphere by setting an attractive table with favorite plates and glasses even if you gathered the meal and didn't cook it yourself. Beauty doesn't take more time to produce than something dull or ordinary. Only have things around you that you love and that are attractive because you should always use your best things when you are together. Who could possibly be more important?

Peter has just invited me to lunch! No matter what, I will not break the date.

ALL HUMAN HISTORY ATTESTS
SINCE EVE ATE APPLES,
MUCH DEPENDS ON DINNER.

Byron

70

Set Aside Times to Sit and Read Together

A MAN OF LEARNING IS NEVER BORED.

Jean Paul Richter

One of the most intimate, loving things partners can do is to sit quietly without distractions, with no interruptions, and read together. When you make this a priority, you can make magical experiences together wherever you are.

Turn off the television. Turn the telephone ringer off. No Internet messaging. Turn off your cell phone. Leave the iPod in another room. Come empty-handed except with what you want to read, a pad of paper and a pen, and something to drink. Reading requires concentration so that you can retain the information and appreciate insights. Listening to soothing background music while studying may improve concentration, but doesn't have the distractions of songs with lyrics. Together select favorite music, or vote for silence.

The busier you are as a couple, the greater the need to share this time together. If one of you talks on the phone, the other's concentration is diminished. New research on the human brain's hundred billion neurons and hundreds of trillions of synaptic connections estimates that it takes us approximately fifteen minutes to regain our focus after an interruption. The brain is a "cognitive powerhouse," as Steve Lohr wrote in a front-page *New York Times* article about the mistakes people make when they multitask. A neuroscientist, René Marois, cites the cause of such errors: "But a core limitation is an inability to concentrate on two things at once." Remember that!

Read whatever you are inclined to. We all save clippings from newspapers; there are magazine articles we want to read; there are books galore. Whether it is a recipe you are curious about or a book on learning how to clear clutter, this is free time, alone together, to read. When Peter and I were engaged, we read fiction together—Hemingway, Henry Miller, Anaïs Nin, D. H. Lawrence, Lawrence Durrell and his brother Henry. We'd mark each other's books and end up in intimate discussions about the big question, "What's the meaning of life?" As an interior designer, I also devoured design, architecture, and art books, and Peter continued to study history, current affairs, and the law, as well as criminal justice.

The *Book of Common Prayer* instructs: "Read, mark, learn and inwardly digest." None of us is born wise. Through reading, studying, travel, and experience we grow in understanding of what is true, right, and lasting. Common sense is not all that common, but when we read together and share ideas, we grow into acquiring better judgment and develop a wider frame of reference.

Learning makes us young no matter how old we are. We can stave off the "blunting influence of old age" (as Aristotle said) by being still, getting ourselves centered, and being together in peace and pleasure to read. These times we set aside are sacred. They lead to connection and an expanded experience of our intimacy. Sharing reading time and space opens us up to spontaneously want to read something out loud. But don't break the spell. Wait to mutually discuss your enthusiasm over dinner. If you have children, you can't imagine the powerful example you'll set for them as they witness the joy of learning, of reading and writing.

Because humans are an intellectual species, when we use our minds to grow in knowledge and understanding, we're using the "muscle" of our brain and it gives us wondrously great pleasure. I know several couples who have an unfortunate disparity in their individual intellectual development. Partners should equally work on their *own* development no matter how great the demands on their time. We should constantly develop our own mind. Then, when we're together, at certain prearranged times, mutual pleasure naturally unfolds.

Being together to read has opened Peter and me to greater understanding of each other's personalities, interests, and talents. We have heated conversations about a wide range of topics and we each expand the other in sharing history, biography, poetry, and even Zen study. Wherever you are, you can make a date to grow closer in understanding as you become wiser. Read together to feel intimately connected. It is a pastime you will never regret.

LET EVERY MAN, IF POSSIBLE,
GATHER SOME GOOD BOOKS UNDER
HIS ROOF.

William Ellery Channing

Stimulate Your Curiosity

CURIOSITY IS ONE OF THE
PERMANENT AND CERTAIN
CHARACTERISTICS OF A VIGOROUS MIND.

Samuel Johnson

We were born as learning sponges. I've never met a normal child who is not curious. I consider myself fortunate to have gone to design school and taken a trip around the world instead of graduating from a liberal arts college. I, as a result, always study. It takes discipline and concentration to begin my day reading Aristotle, or his teacher Plato, but I'm not intimidated; I'm curious and impressed by how fresh and relevant ancient wisdom is to our lives today.

My serious studies have nothing to do with becoming an intellectual. I'm simply drawn to abstract, philosophical thought. I study transcendentalism, existentialism, and metaphysics. I'm curious about what people believe, how they think and feel and live. My exposure to different cultures around the world has made me curious about their unique customs, myths, and lifestyles. I try to continually stimulate my curiosity by reading and traveling. Peter and I have grown more inquisitive each day. We're eager to learn about completely divergent points of view. We have open minds, not afraid to reconsider our thinking.

Everyone has some sense of curiosity but many of us are too lazy to follow through on our inner promptings. Or we let life impediments—chores, children, or work—get in the way. But the more curious and interested in a wide variety of things we are, the more interesting we become to our partners. What are some things you're currently curious about? What do you want to learn?

learn a language
read *War and Peace*
learn to tap dance
research a specific issue
learn about Chinese art
take voice lessons
study astronomy or astrology
take a writing course
go to interior design school
study watercolor
take a cooking class by a French chef
learn how to quilt
take up golf
go on a spiritual retreat
write your autobiography
study flower arranging

When you become curious about something, pursue it immediately. Don't put it off. Look things up in the dictionary, the encyclopedia, or on the Internet. Browse in a bookstore and select a book or two that "calls" to you. Once started, strive to accomplish a course of action. Have learning be your favorite hobby.

Confucius said, "What is most needed for learning is a humble mind." A favorite saying of the great master Michelangelo was, "I am still learning." Curiosity is unlimited, available to us twenty-four hours a day—at no cost. Ask questions, big questions: What should I do with my time on earth? Be curious also about the mundane. Ask why? How? Be interested in everything that will enrich your happiness and satisfaction. The more you learn and know about the way the world works, the more you will want to learn. Socrates confessed to Plato, "All I know is that I know nothing." The more you think, the more you have to think about.

Audit courses at universities. My editor has a friend whose husband, after auditing classes, has enrolled in theology school—at age seventy! He is blissfully happy—and his wife is happy for *him*. He's taking his time to savor the process and has mapped out a plan to be finished at the age of seventy-seven! Don't be afraid of not being able to prove yourself. Albert Einstein reminds us, "The most beautiful thing we can experience is the mysterious. It is the source of all true art and science." He warned us not to make the intellect our god: "It has, of course, powerful muscles, but no personality." Your curiosity sparks your personality, providing boundless variety to your full measure of happiness.

HAPPY THE MAN WHO COULD
SEARCH OUT THE CAUSES OF THINGS.

Virgil

Kindness and Diplomacy Win Hearts and Minds

LET US BE, FIRST AND ABOVE ALL,
KIND, THEN HONEST, AND THEN
LET US NEVER FORGET EACH OTHER,
AND MAY THE MEMORY LIVE ETERNALLY.

Fyodor Mikhaylovich Dostoyevsky

The diplomacy of kindness is the single most important character trait possible among a committed couple. The Roman Stoic philosopher Seneca had a great insight: "We should live our lives as if everyone could see us, as if the most secret corners of our soul were open to the sight of others . . . All divine and human learning can be summarized in one truth—that we are members of one big body. Nature unites us in one big family, and we should live our lives together, helping each other." Let us as committed partners be kinder and more gentle to each other. Seneca also reminds us that "wherever there is a human being there is a chance for a kindness."

I was surprised to learn from my informal research on character traits that kindness was not rated number one. Honesty was the virtue most people admired in other people's character or what they value in their own strengths. Honesty is fundamental. Are too many people today untrustworthy? None of us appreciates being lied to or cheated.

What characteristics do you most admire in your partner? Kindness, thoughtfulness, empathy, consideration, and caring are most important to me. If your lover is kind, generous, warmhearted, loving, friendly, outgoing, and forgiving, you will live your lives together in harmony and contentment. When we are kind to each other we are gentle and sensitive and have a humble demeanor, showing sympathy and understanding.

Kindness is not as common a virtue as we'd like it to be. Perhaps, sadly, it is not a gift every human being possesses. Peter is always honorable and fair to me and because he is kindhearted, he intuitively wants what is best for me. Peter and I are drawn to kind people. We put a high value on kindness as do our friends and heroes. The Talmud teaches, "The highest wisdom is kindness." Some wise souls go so far as to believe kindness to be their religion. When we value kindness, we speak and act with a soft touch. Think of the different ways to share kind behavior between couples:

caregiving
respect in private as well as in public
fundamental respect and honoring of each other
trusting each other
offering compassion and understanding
being aware and paying attention to your partner's
  needs at all times
recognizing the unity between you and your partner

Kindness is the essential virtue of your enlightenment. Sensitivity is the essential component of kindness and in turn, love. A major consideration to keep in mind in succeeding in bestowing kindness on your soul mate is the continuous requirement of discipline.

Ask yourself regularly, "How can I be more kind, helpful, and lov-ing to my partner?" The English poet William Wordsworth concludes, "That best portion of a good man's life [is] his little, nameless, unre-membered acts of kindness and of love." Kindness leads to kindness and wins over hearts and minds. The more mutual kindness, the greater your happiness as a couple.

KINDNESS IN WORDS CREATES
CONFIDENCE. KINDNESS IN
THINKING CREATES PROFOUNDNESS.
KINDNESS IN GIVING CREATES LOVE.

Lao Tzu

Live a Little!

Why be dreary? Why be boring? Why get stuck in the rut of ho-hum routine? When I was single I'd call a friend spontaneously and invite her to go to the movies or an art opening or out for supper. Janet was inflexible. Wednesday night she did her hair and nails—toes and fingers—and she couldn't alter her routine.

We all are creatures of habit. We tend to go to the same restaurant and order the same meal over and over. When we discover things we enjoy, we tend to want to repeat the experience because it is a safe bet we'll find it pleasant again. But there are delicious dishes at restaurants that we'll discover if we live a little and dare to go outside of our self-inflicted box.

Peter and I met a cute couple in Stonington Village several years ago who come to stay at the Inn at Stonington three times a year. On every visit, they go to a favorite restaurant a few miles away on the Rhode Island border for dinner on Saturday night. They each order coquilles St. Jacques. This is a tradition. They don't even listen to the waiter telling them about the specials. Evelyn and Bob have been married forty-eight years. Soon after Bob retired, he wanted to kick up his heels a little and over breakfast he suggested, "Let's go out for lunch today." Evelyn automatically responded, "I can't. I have to go grocery shopping." When a spouse retires, a couple should rethink everything in order to live a little. Under changed circumstances, everything changes.

Take regular breaks from your routine. Life is too valuable to limit your enjoyment because of self-imposed habits that are all about maintenance, not living richly in the moment.

Be receptive to serendipitous discoveries. When we act spontaneously, we generate more excitement and pleasure. It's fine to make plans, but we shouldn't become rigid. Some of the happiest times in my life have been when I've been swept away from my duties. For our overall well-being, we need to take breaks from our work, even when we're under a deadline. I remember with great happiness Peter coming to a public library where I was writing and whispering in my ear, "You look hungry. Take a break." And I did.

It's a virtue to be conscientious, but we can overdo our work ethic. In order for us to be at our creative best, we need variety and breaks from the routine of our daily lives. Splurge and have more treats. Together, walk to a café for coffee and a sweet. Go on more dates together. Take a car ride to see the fall foliage. Visit the botanical gardens. Attend a jazz concert. Rather than going home and scratching around in the freezer for something to heat in the microwave, call your love from work and meet at a nearby Thai restaurant. Live with a sense of abundance, not scarcity. Money should be saved, not hoarded; it's a tool and can be wisely used to notch up one's sense of liveliness and happiness.

Live a little: "I accept. What fun. What a treat."

I COULD HAVE DANCED ALL NIGHT!

Alan Jay Lerner

Me & You

UNITED WE STAND,
DIVIDED WE FALL.

Aesop

We're born alone and we die alone. We're really fortunate to have a soul mate to share our joys and to grow through the difficult times. Life is impermanent. We all are going to die. When you or your lover are going through a crisis, you come down to absolute fundamentals. This is the secret answer: In times of extreme challenge, turn directly to each other where resolution and solace are found.

Last spring Peter and I enjoyed lunch at a favorite bistro before attending an exhibition of paintings by Claude Monet at a nearby gallery. That evening we were going to fly to Paris to celebrate our anniversary—a tradition that becomes more sentimental each year. Suddenly a friend appeared at the restaurant and shared a sip of wine with us before her guest arrived. Roxanne Coady is a brilliant, creative visionary. Our few serendipitous minutes together were electrifying. Roxanne owns the welcoming bookstore R. J. Julia in Madison, Connecticut. I asked her if she could think of a title for my new book. Silence; then her eyes flashed, and she spoke: "*Me & You.*" Seconds later she was off to another table with her lunch date.

While *Me & You* did not become the title of this book, it is the ultimate secret to happiness for two. Peter and I are in the habit now of saying *Me & You* to each other to remind ourselves that no matter what happens around us or to us, we have each other. This won't last forever. We understand that our partnership will someday end because of death, but while we are both alive we have found our other half and together we are whole. One individual joins another individual. You share each other. You learn to love each other more deeply when you stick together, are intimate and enjoy seamless love.

Me & You. By strengthening your higher self, you give substance to your partnership. Peter and I are best friends. We completely rely on each other. The key is to turn to each other first. We let ourselves rely on each other to pull us through whatever challenges we face. Life is serious. We know from our own experience that everyone is struggling in some way. There is always a dark spot in the sunshine of life because no one knows anything concrete about their future. By turning toward each other, you grow through your serious situations and literally become closer through them. By seeking wisdom and comfort from your other half, you are both lifted up. You're able to talk things out, encourage each other, be a cheerleader when appropriate.

Whenever I'm in a crisis, I count on Peter not only to protect me but to tell me I can do it, I'm strong, I can figure things out. No one else, not one other human being, knows your whole situation. Other people protect themselves when they give free advice. I've discovered that people can be extremely awkward and negative when they are invited into a situation that should be solved between two people alone. Whether you are under the gun of an impossible deadline, are sad because a loved one is dying, or have been given a bad diagnosis, rather than turning to a trusted friend or professional or turning inward, face the painful circumstance together privately in the intimacy of your sacred bond.

You will find your support and strengthen each other by acknowledging no other resource is better to lean on than your partner. A young

194 • Alexandra Stoddard

couple from a close-knit family in the Midwest went to Japan for a year because of a business opportunity. There they were with a six-month-old baby in the heart of Tokyo not knowing the language, having no friends, with no support system in place except each other. When they left for Japan, they had no idea how close they could become. This, they both agreed, would form the depth of their union throughout their lifetime together.

Be prepared for other people to express doubts about your mutual decisions or activities. When you both come to a decision to sell your house or move to Arizona, it is really none of anyone's business if it is right for the two of you.

Me & You celebrating the world. You are a blessed team participating in the drama of life. When the going gets rough, you must already have this secret understanding in place.

When you are in unison, when you rely on and trust each other, nothing will ever be overwhelming. Some men are reluctant to open up to face their emotions, but there is such richness to be had when you can share your feelings with your lover and come to trust the fact that you are both blessed and you don't have to face anything all by yourself. Turn toward your partner in all difficult situations and know that you have these confidences available when a crisis looms. Going the extra mile together is deepening. While you have each other, love each other. *Me & You.* Love & Live Happy. You have your best friend to turn to, your second self.

A FRIEND IS A SECOND SELF.

Aristotle

75

Your Happiness Is Up to You

HAPPINESS DEPENDS UPON OURSELVES.

Aristotle

We can't give love and happiness from a hollow heart. We can't give what we don't have. We grow in wisdom from living life fully, and the only way we can cultivate the spirit of joy together is to value our own life. Erich Fromm explained, "Appetite is a phenomenon of abundance; its satisfaction not a necessity but an expression of freedom and productiveness. The pleasure accompanying it may be called joy."

Often, when I'm in an audience, I ask people to evaluate their setpoint for happiness on a daily basis by assigning a score from one to ten, with ten being the greatest amount of happiness possible. Peter always volunteers that from one to ten, his is "twelve." Giggles follow; sometimes people clap and laugh out loud. Peter also observes that he's always naturally been a happy person, but feels he has gone from ten to twelve in his maturity. I am witness to this dependable happiness Peter radiates every day.

People aren't as happy at home as they'd like others to believe they are, I've discovered in my interior design work. Because of this discovery, I've devoted a great deal of time and energy to studying happiness. My research indicates a compelling argument that happiness comes from within. Our mind and heart, our feelings, make us truly happy—not things, status, power, or money. No matter how fortunate we are, if we're not thankful for the gifts we have, we will not be happy.

In order to attain greater, more lasting, dependable happiness, we must continue to look inward. Peter and I share research, we read the works of the great philosophers, we travel the country leading happiness retreats. From all our work and travel, we have learned that the more people pay attention to their *own* happiness, the greater their awareness of their own needs and desires, the better able they are to do whatever is necessary to fulfill themselves and be in a position to help others.

It is an interesting experience to wake up in the morning and make up your mind to be happy. When you do, you live in an entirely different consciousness than someone who waits for happiness from outside events, susceptible to all the negative energy in the world.

Isn't it liberating to think that you don't have to have a reason to be happy? Happiness can come naturally to you. Don't let life's complexities interfere with your own and your lover's happiness. You can't live a frenetic life and grow in wisdom. Read the headlines: "Busy lives keep women sleep-deprived: 'Biological need' ranks low on priority lists." People become depressed when they are sleep-deprived. To make matters worse, they may overconsume sugary foods and use medication to keep them alert.

Rely on your common sense. Do we really have to go to the gym at 5:30 A.M. and send e-mail messages from bed all hours of the night? Where is the Golden Mean of excellence between too little and too much? Isn't the bed where you come together to touch, where you talk, and where you spend one-third of your lives together? According to a survey by the National Association of Home Builders, architects predict that more than 60 percent of custom homes will have separate master bedrooms by 2015.

The *New York Times* recently reported in an article entitled "Too Busy to Notice You're Too Busy" that psychiatrist (and author of *Crazy Busy: Overstretched, Overbooked and About to Snap*) Edward M. Hallowell knew he had "crossed into the dark side from busy to crazy busy when he got mad at a rotary phone while staying at a vacation house." To dial took a mere eleven seconds. He'd become a man in a hurry even when he had no need to hurry. Hallowell writes about the overlapping reasons "we all fall into the trap of being overly busy. We touch away on cell phones and BlackBerrys. We avoid dealing with life's big issues—death, global warming, AIDS, terrorism—by running from task to task. We do not know how not to be busy."

There is no reason to go mad with busy-ness. Don't fall into this trap where you snuff out your life force, become breathless, and forget about your own personal happiness. Don't get caught up in compromising your self. To live exuberantly, you can't be exhausted and frustrated. Choose the goal of happiness: That is your success. Maintain a good spirit.

The secrets for finding more joy together are in both your hearts. Lasting happiness for two, to a great extent, is up to you.

NO HUMAN BEING CAN
REALLY UNDERSTAND ANOTHER,
AND NO ONE CAN ARRANGE
ANOTHER'S HAPPINESS.

Graham Greene

Afterword

When two happy souls become lovers, both partners can continuously find more joy together by paying attention. This principle is simple but not always easy because it requires us to be mindful of our *own* faults, our own character weaknesses.

When seeking greater happiness for two, we assume the responsibility of working on ourselves, learning more about our intentions and our strengths and how best to eliminate our shortcomings. In order for our love to be pure, we should remove obstacles that interfere with our capacity to give and receive unconditional love.

When Peter and I met, I was thirteen. I've looked up to him ever since. Peter and I give each other undivided attention whenever possible. We try not to rush. We want to fully appreciate each other's company and savor our experiences. Neither of us enjoys multitasking because we know from experience it makes us mindless, anxious, and numb.

From observation, a vast majority of people who desperately want to be in control are *out* of control. By being mindful of the purity of your love, you will value the excellence of this relationship that only you and your lover will ever know fully or understand. Your mutual love can be a powerful force for good.

I wake up every morning with a great desire to live joyfully. I've learned a lot over these fifty-four years since Peter and I met. I know that it is my job to improve myself; I am the only person I can change. I believe the fact that I don't want to change Peter and he doesn't want to change me is the secret of our love happiness together. We love each other just as we are.

When my publisher asked Peter to write the Foreword to *Happiness for Two*, I was touched by his sublime words. My greatest wish for you is that each day you find your love for each other increases, and that you achieve great happiness for you and the love of your life.

"LOVE & LIVE HAPPY"

Alexandra Stoddard

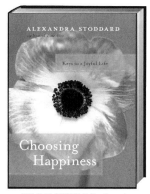

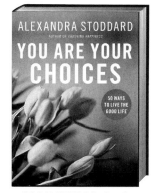